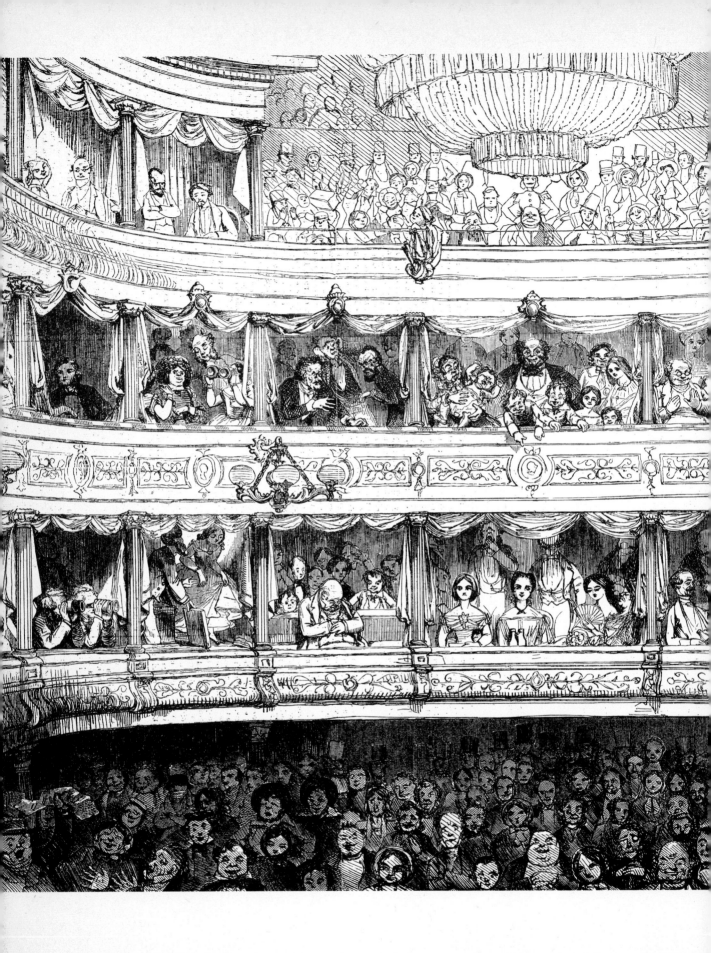

VICTOR GLASSTONE

Victorian and Edwardian Theatres

AN ARCHITECTURAL AND
SOCIAL SURVEY
with 210 illustrations
8 in colour

THAMES AND HUDSON
LONDON

For my mother

Half-title page

Theatre Royal, Chatham, 1900. Architect: G. E. Bond
(decorated by A. R. Dean). A cherub from the front of the
dress circle photographed in 1956, shortly before the theatre
was dismantled. The structure remains as the premises of
a car-hire firm.

Frontispiece

'The Pantomime from the Clown's Point of View'. An
engraving from *The Illustrated Times*, 9 January 1858, which
depicts one of the main themes of this book – the audience
in the theatre. Although credited as being of the Theatre
Royal, Drury Lane, the artist used considerable license,
omitting the top tier and gallery, see p. 14.

Printed in Great Britain at the Alden Press, Oxford.

Contents

Foreword and acknowledgments

THE THEATRES of Victorian and Edwardian Britain, after many years of neglect and destruction, have at last been recognized as superb examples of the art of theatre architecture, and their theatrical atmosphere and delightful appearance are finding an ever-widening circle of admirers. This appreciation has been fostered over the last few decades by such bodies of enthusiasts as The Society for Theatre Research and its progeny, the Council for Theatre Preservation, which has since grown and broadened in scope by becoming the Theatres' Advisory Council. The Save London's Theatres Campaign and bands of articulate supporters in the provinces have given momentum to an awareness which has effectively stemmed the tide of demolition responsible for the destruction of so many beautiful theatres and threatening many others at various times.

Despite the renewed interest in theatre architecture of this period, no attempt has so far been made to show how the style, loosely termed Victorian–Edwardian, evolved, flourished and finally declined; nor has anyone considered its particular merits and defects. The aim of this book is to attempt a more systematic consideration of theatre architecture of this period and, in so doing, to gain further converts.

I am grateful to the many libraries, museums and colleagues who have assisted my researches over many years, and to the managements who permitted me to photograph their beautiful theatres. For this book, special mention must be made of Miss Helen Willard, former Curator of the Harvard Theatre Collection; Mr Stephen Croad of the National Monuments Record; the Library of the Royal Institute of British Architects; Mr George Nash and Mr Tony Latham of the Enthoven Collection, Victoria and Albert Museum; Mr Fordham, Chatham Library; Mr Rupert Rhymes of the English National Opera, London Coliseum; Mr Warren Smith of the Leeds Grand Theatre and Opera House Ltd; Mr John Tooley of the Royal Opera House, Covent Garden; Mr John Hallett of Theatres Consolidated Ltd; Mr Ian Albery of The Wyndham Theatres Ltd; the Abbey Theatre, Dublin; Howard and Wyndham Ltd; Manchester Palace of Varieties Ltd; Richmond Theatre Ltd; Mr David Cheshire and Mr Iain Mackintosh. My particular thanks are also due to Mr Leonard Schach and Mr John Malcolm Brinnin.

The modern photographs were taken by the author. All illustrations come from his own archive, with the exception of the following: *2*, from the British Museum, London; *6*, from the Henry E. Huntington Library and Art Gallery, California; *3*, from Richard Leacroft; *1*, from the Cabinet des Dessins, the Louvre, Paris; *48*, from Eric de Maré; *40, 76, 79, 94, 95, 109, 113, 115, 116, 117, 118, 146, 148, 149, 151, 153, 154, 155, 156, 157, 158, 160, 161, 162, 163, 166, 167, 187, 188, 189, 190, 191, 194, 195, 196, 197, 198, 200, 202*, from the National Monuments Record, London; *21*, from the South African Library, Cape Town; *30*, from *The Times*, London; *4, 5, 9, 18, 56*, from the Enthoven Collection, Victoria and Albert Museum, London.

Introduction

THEATRE ARCHITECTURE during Victoria's reign and the first two decades of the twentieth century is one of the summits of achievement reached by this fascinating and highly specialized architectural form, matched only during the Classical Greek and Continental Baroque periods.

Curiously enough, the times of greatest achievement in theatre architecture have not always been those which produced the finest dramatic writing. Theatre architecture is linked to the social climate of a period, its aspirations and sense of corporate stability, because it is a social art. Whereas the Baroque theatre building reflects the opera of its day – and has, indeed, been described as 'frozen opera' – the Greek theatres were not formalized in *stone* until long after the great classical dramatists were dead; they were, in fact, academic theatres created for an established repertory of plays. The nineteenth century repeats this pattern. Despite the great operas that were being composed on the Continent, playwriting everywhere was at a particularly low ebb, yet many great plays from the past were available for performance and new ones, contrary to our present critical view, were very popular with contemporary audiences. Theatrical vitality does not necessarily depend on the quality of its dramatic literature, nor on high standards of presentation; even today the best plays do not usually attract the largest audiences. And in our time, of course, the theatre as a form of entertainment has to compete with other media, while in the nineteenth century it reigned supreme.

It could be argued that by the end of the last century dramatic literature had reached great heights, matching the brilliance of the theatre building itself, then in its maturity; that the two forms were for a brief period developing in unison. Yet there was a divergence of aim between theatre architects and dramatists. The architects were concerned with creating a suitably stimulating environment for all levels of society and were completely at one with that society's standards and ambitions, whereas the greatest dramatists, including Ibsen, Shaw, Chekhov and Wilde, were determined to reform as well as entertain, either by polemic or by satire. They were not concerned about changing theatre architecture. The buildings they had suited them perfectly; they also suited the actors and the singers and were a perfect setting for the audiences that flocked into them. Change, when it came in the first decades of the twentieth century, was generated by scene-designers like Craig and Appia, and by theatre directors like Reinhardt and Taïrov. They in their turn were developing and expanding the revolutionary ideas of the one composer and dramatist who *did* concern himself with the form and conception of the theatre building, Wagner.

With this one exception, throughout the nineteenth century all those concerned with the theatre agreed that it was a place of magic and illusion, of entertainment and enchantment, and this attitude mirrored the feelings of a satisfied audience. In this climate of general accord, theatre architects could create masterpieces of fantasy, instinct with an atmosphere and a superb handling of space which were theatrical in all senses of the word; the theatre was indeed a place for the 'suspension of disbelief'.

Although this book concerns itself, for reasons of space, economy and unity, only with Britain and the British Empire, the nineteenth and early twentieth centuries were, throughout the Western world, periods of supreme fulfilment for the art of theatre architecture. The tradition of the parent country influenced the theatres in the Empires of France, Germany, Italy, Spain, Portugal, Russia and Central European countries; theatre in North America, like that in the Empires, went its own way, inevitably open to cross-influences and interactions, but nevertheless reflecting its own particular culture and architecture.

Britain and France differed from other countries in having long traditions of centralized government; hence the importance of theatres in their capital cities, London and Paris. But there the similarity ends. From the seventeenth century Paris had a tradition of state subsidy to the theatre, whereas London had none. Certainly, companies of actors entertained at court, where, naturally, they were paid; they also received both Royal and noble patronage and, later, charters to perform. Theatres to which on occasion the public was admitted (on payment, as at a regular theatre) were erected at court, particularly in the Stuart and Caroline periods, but they were temporary or short-lived. This situation differed markedly from that of the subsidized and permanent theatres erected by the many tiny courts of Germany, Italy and other Continental countries during the Baroque period. In the eighteenth and nineteenth centuries, with the growing power of the middle classes, subsidized theatre was taken over by civic authorities who competed, as the courts had done, in building ever more costly and elaborate theatres. These subsidized buildings existed side by side with commercial theatres which, of necessity, were cramped and less opulent.

The tradition in Britain, and later in North America, was quite different. Lacking state or civic subsidy, the commercial theatre flourished or floundered at the public's whim. Profit was the spur. The buildings were, as a result, makeshift and, until the end of the eighteenth century, inexpensively constructed, particularly outside London. Yet within these simple and often gimcrack houses there developed a dramatic tradition second to none. Opera, derivative of developments abroad, always lagged behind, being something of a poor relation – definitely not part of the national genius. After the Puritan theatre-hating interregnum, the Charters, the Letters Patent given by Charles II in 1662 to Thomas Killigrew for Drury Lane and to Sir William Davenant for Lincoln's Inn Fields, 'whence it descended in 1732 via Dorset Garden to Covent Garden', gave Drury Lane and Covent Garden the sole right to perform drama. These theatres became known as the Patent Theatres. The musical theatre, on the other hand, was free to all who could obtain the necessary licences. This peculiarly British combination of control, *laissez faire* and commercialism is closely reflected in the design of the theatres themselves. In the eighteenth century they were of minimal scale and comfort, and were particularly adapted to the spoken word. Although music was always part of the theatre, the performance of opera *per se* was incidental, and

London gained its first opera house, the Queen's, almost by accident in 1705. This theatre (later to become the King's, Her Majesty's and His Majesty's, according to the sex of the reigning monarch) was conceived by its famous architect/playwright/owner Sir John Vanbrugh as 'a triumphal piece of architecture'; but, as critics of the day commented, 'not one word can be distinctly heard'. It was therefore suitable for nothing *but* opera, and had to be altered many times before it was acoustically adequate even for that.

This ambiguity and uncertainty of function is typical of the British theatre building throughout its history. Even the Theatres Royal, the two Patent Theatres, were used for every imaginable theatrical activity, as well as many civic ones such as meetings, balls, banquets and fêtes, while the minor theatres, prevented by law from staging straight drama, *had* to resort to musical interludes, sometimes lasting only a few minutes, in order to be allowed to present a play. It was always necessary to obtain licences to perform but, after the 1843 Act which abolished the drama monopoly, it was comparatively easy to switch from one kind of licence to another. Consequently, a theatre built as a drama house could go over to opera or music hall or vice versa within months of its opening. Sometimes a few adjustments were made to the building, but quite often only the name was changed.

As improvisation and change have always been one of the strengths of the British theatre, the material presented in this book has not been organized according to building types, playhouses, opera houses and music halls, but is treated thematically and chronologically. An attempt has been made to show the most intrinsic and significant aspects and changes of each decade, with the emphasis on the atmosphere from the point of view of the audience, something which in turn affected the actor's attitude to his craft.

The architecture of the theatre is related to current fashions in secular architecture generally. Curiously enough, however, historians concerned with theatre buildings tend not to view their subject in the light of *stylistic* changes in

architecture, concentrating instead on the actor/audience relationship and on the history of staging and performance. Unfortunately, space here does not allow for more than an occasional glance at stage machinery; this subject has been treated fully in other books, some of which are mentioned in the bibliography.

The pattern of the post-Renaissance British theatre, and the social and economic changes which affected its physical aspect, are well illustrated in the history of its most famous playhouse and all-purpose theatre, the Theatre Royal, Drury Lane. Here on one site, in five buildings, with their innumerable redecorations and partial reconstructions, can be seen almost every form and change which took place during a period of more than three centuries. At one time or another Drury Lane has taken on the shape, style and ambition of almost every indoor theatre erected in the kingdom, with the exception, of course, of those built since the 1930s.

Although it is quite impossible adequately to condense the long history of this important theatre, some indication of its changes will be a helpful background to the theme of this book. Readers who wish to know more are strongly recommended to consult the *Survey of London*, vol. XXXV, 'The Theatre Royal, Drury Lane, and the Royal Opera House, Covent Garden', and Richard Leacroft's *The Development of the English Playhouse*.

Situated in a busy and highly populated built-up area of London, the first theatre to appear on the site was in the middle of what is virtually an island block. The ground was, and still is, owned by the Earls (now Dukes) of Bedford, and the theatre was a temporary structure erected in 1635. Little is known of it save that it took seventeen days to build and was 'a playhouse 31 foote broad & 40 foote longe; boarded walles and sheded with pann tiles'. By this description and the fact that it was licensed by the Lord Chamberlain to a group of French players, it is reasonable to suppose that it was of the simplest kind; a rectangle with a raised stage and with maybe a single gallery around three of its sides, such as that seen in the drawing by Abraham Bosse of a French theatre of *c.* 1630 (*1*).

This type of small auditorium, somewhat elaborated and with a lower stage, was built in English country towns in the eighteenth and early nineteenth centuries; a charming example dating from 1788 still exists in Richmond, Yorkshire. It was also, in essence, the form of the tavern music halls of the 1840s and 1850s (see pp. 44, 45).

Killigrew's was the next theatre to be erected on the site, which had in the meantime become known as the 'Rideing Yard'. The first to be known as the Theatre Royal, it opened on 7 May 1663 and was twice the size of its predecessor. The leasehold ground, still hemmed in by other buildings, measured 112 feet by 58–9 feet. Pepys commented that the theatre was 'of extraordinary good contrivance, and yet hath some faults, as the narrowness of the passages in and out of the pitt, and the distance from the stage to boxes, which I am confident cannot hear'. M. de Monconys, 'visiting the theatre on 22 May 1663, thought it to be the most proper and most beautiful he had ever seen, much of it lined with green baize. The boxes were dressed with bands of gilt leather, and the benches of the pit, where persons of quality resorted, were ranged in the form of an amphitheatre, each higher than the one in front.'

During the plague of 1665 the theatre was altered slightly and the stage enlarged. The next description came in 1669 from an Italian, Magalotti, who noted that 'this theatre is nearly of a circular form, surrounded, in the inside, by boxes separated from each other, and divided into several rows of seats, for the greater accommodation of the ladies, who, in conformity with the freedom of the country, sit together indiscriminately: a large space being left on the ground floor for the rest of the audience'. No iconography exists for this first

2

Theatre Royal. Some scholars have tried to associate a sheet of very inconclusive sketches by Sir Christopher Wren with the building, but they are quite unlike the contemporary descriptions, and Wren is not known to have had anything to do with this Drury Lane. However, his still extant Sheldonian Theatre, Oxford, built in 1664–7, does fit the descriptions very well indeed. Much influenced by sixteenth-century interpretations of Vitruvius, and by the theatres of Serlio and Palladio, the building was designed as the principal assembly-room of the University, and not as a regular theatre. As seen in this water colour of 1781 by S. H. Grimm (2), one can gain from the Sheldonian some idea of the *atmosphere* of the first and second Theatres Royal.

The 'first' theatre was destroyed by fire on 25 January 1672, and the 'second' (the 1635 temporary structure is not normally included in numbering the Theatres Royal, Drury Lane, 1–4) opened on 26 March 1674, lasting structurally, despite numerous redecorations and rebuildings, until 1791. Again, a sectional and far more detailed drawing by Wren has been associated with the 1674 building, this time far more convincingly. Although the only contemporary allusion to the great architect's involvement was made by Colley Cibber who, in criticizing the alterations made about 1690, commented that 'it were but Justice to lay the

original Figure, which Sir Christopher Wren gave it', various historians have argued that the dimensions of the Wren section agree very well with those of the known site. Richard Leacroft, working back from the beautiful drawings and engravings which exist for Robert Adam's reconstruction of 1775, is convinced that the original 'second' theatre had the splayed walls which the 'second' Drury Lane is known to have had in its last years. The fan shape

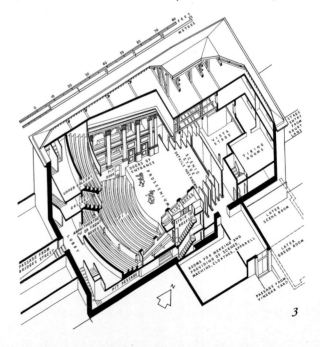

3

was also used in the eighteenth-century plans of the Queen's and of Covent Garden, and was peculiar at the time to the British theatre. It would have added to the effect of the perspective scenes which were used on the stage. Leacroft's reconstruction (3) shows the deep forestage and double proscenium doors, much beloved by English actors, which appear in Wren's drawing. The boxes above these doors, and in the splayed walls, are contained within a giant order of Corinthian pilasters, very reminiscent of the Schouwburg, Amsterdam, of 1637.

The second Drury Lane was still encased, like its predecessor, by surrounding buildings and could be approached only down two narrow passages, one at the front for the audience, another at the back for the actors. The 'front of house' accommodation was of the barest minimum, limited to access staircases and cramped corridors behind the shallow balconies. Over the years, this situation was improved slightly by the addition of further passages from the surrounding streets and by the acquisition of rooms from adjacent buildings. The forestage was repeatedly reduced in depth, and the double proscenium doors were replaced by stage boxes, single proscenium doors being created on the scene stage. In 1762 Garrick forbade spectators the right to sit on the stage, and to compensate for this the capacity of the house was increased. Somehow or other, about 2,000 people were squeezed onto the benches which filled this relatively small theatre. By modern standards it must have been acutely uncomfortable and unbearably stuffy!

Robert Adam's famous reconstruction of 1775 improved matters slightly. Everything was made lighter and airier, in feeling if not in fact, because the basic structure remained. The ceiling over the now much reduced forestage was heightened, and the stage opening widened. Plate glass over coloured foil was used to face the slender square-shafted wooden columns which supported the tiers. Ornament, in Adam's typical manner, gave the house a crisp elegance. The Adam–Pastorini engraving (4) shows Drury Lane to have had a very different character from Continental theatres of the same period, although the human figures scaled

down to almost half-size create a false impression of immensity. The forestage, for instance, was only 30 feet wide.

Most dramatically, however, Drury Lane had at last acquired a façade (5)! Over the years, various leases of the small properties flanking the theatre had been acquired, so that exit from all four sides was now possible. The stage had grown 100 feet deeper and scene shops, etc., were added to the sides of the theatre. Most important, the entire area between the back of the auditorium and Bridges (now Catherine) Street was given over to lobbies and entrance passages. Adam was now enabled to create a dignified Georgian frontispiece of Ionic pilasters and pediment surmounting the various entrances, each of which led to a separate part of the house.

Polite society could now reach their boxes without the embarrassment of jostling with people of the rougher sort.

Adam's reconstruction was widely praised in 1775, but by 1783 his decoration was considered stale and gaudy, and the theatre was done over. The wide boxes were subdivided and enclosed, becoming, in the words of a contemporary critic, 'a nest for prostitutes of both sexes'. They were opened up again in 1785, and two years later the theatre was again redecorated. By 1791, however, it had become too old and too small for London's growing needs; rather than yield his monopoly position to demands for a third drama theatre, Richard Brinsley Sheridan, who was now in control, decided to rebuild completely. The company moved into the King's, the second Drury Lane was demolished and Henry Holland commenced the long, expensive and frustrating business of designing and erecting the third theatre.

By now, the entire island site was available, enabling the architect to consider constructing a magnificent colonnaded building which would vie with the grandiose theatres of Continental cities. But funds ran out and when the theatre opened on 12 March 1794 the splendid edifice, which was to have comprised not only a theatre at the back but taverns, coffee-houses, houses and shops in the front, was incomplete. It remained so, only the theatre part being ever built. Instead of the great front elevation envisaged by Holland, a boarded-up empty site greeted the audience.

The inside, however, was very fine (6). In line with Continental practice, the auditorium was now horseshoe-shaped. Five tiers of open boxes towered above a steeply raked floor of pit benches. Facing the stage, the tiers continued back and up to form an immense two-shilling gallery and, even higher, a far distant shilling gallery. The house, seating 3,919, had the greatest capacity in Europe, although this figure was achieved by allowing 14 inches per person in the pit, and 18 inches in the more expensive box seats. The stage too was vast, with a proscenium opening 43 feet wide by 38 feet high. The cost of filling this great space with painted scenery was crippling, and Sheridan was perpetually in debt.

By 1797, the stage opening was narrowed by inserting a column of stage boxes above the proscenium doors (omitted from the original scheme, to the anger of the actors), and lowered by a new sounding board which, it was hoped, would improve the bad acoustics. Drury Lane was now too large for the spoken word.

Holland, despite the old theatre's excellent record of 117 fire-free years, was acutely aware of the potential danger. He provided an iron safety curtain and great water tanks above the stage. Much of the timberwork was protected by 'Fire Plates' and other fireproof gadgets. But the safety curtain rusted and was removed; and on the night of 24 February 1809, when the theatre caught fire, the water tanks were practically empty. Next morning, barely the shell of the building remained standing. Sheridan was ruined.

Nonetheless, eternally optimistic, within months he had conjured up a scheme for rebuilding. Committees were formed, and an Act of Parliament was passed; but by April 1810 Sheridan found himself excluded from his own project. Samuel Whitbread, the brewer, now led a joint-stock company ('the first to be established in the London theatre business') of 86 noblemen and gentlemen, and Benjamin Dean Wyatt was commissioned to design the fourth Drury Lane. The first stone was laid on 29 October 1811, and the theatre which opened on 10 October 1812 remains to this day. The splendid foyers, staircases and noble rotunda in the late Georgian Classical style are virtually intact as the architect designed them (7).

Although Wyatt was intensely aware of theatre developments abroad and wished to compete with the spacious and self-contained theatres of Continental cities, his building was stylistically very

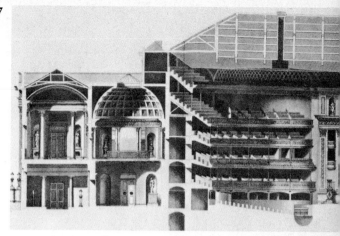

English. The plan of a circular auditorium, entered from grandiose foyers and surrounded by dressing-rooms and administrative offices, all facing the stage with its workshops and scene docks, could be any one of many similar schemes found in Paris, Bordeaux, Berlin or Milan; but the decorative effect differed considerably. The charming little Chinese canopy over the first tier of dress boxes and the entire proscenium arch treatment are essentially of Regency England. The façade too, with a simplicity dictated by economy, is in the Neo-classical style as interpreted during the English Greek Revival (8). The present portico was added in 1820 and the elegant Grecian Ionic colonnade in Russell Street, with its fluted shafts made of cast iron, appeared in 1831.

Cast and wrought iron were also used extensively throughout Wyatt's theatre. Thin cast-iron columns supported the iron construction of the balconies and staircases and, in a further attempt to combat the fire hazard, water sprinklers were fitted in all parts of the house. Yet, despite the architect's serious attempts to design the perfect theatre, dissatisfaction was soon voiced, particularly by the actors, who were still harping on the loss of their precious proscenium doors – a feature which Wyatt had considered ridiculous, and one which would have spoiled the effect of the proscenium arch's being 'what the frame of a Picture is to the Picture itself': a very early use of this analogy and one which was contrary to British stage practice (9). But the actors won, and in 1814 the columns which formed the sides of Wyatt's picture frame were replaced by proscenium doors. His tiny proscenium boxes, which had been angled away from any possible view of what went on within his picture frame, were replaced by a range of four boxes which had a slightly better view. The entire house was redecorated at the same time, 'for in a Theatre novelty has an undisputed sway'. Another redecoration was carried out in 1819.

By 1822 it was realized that Wyatt's 33-foot proscenium was too narrow for the width of the house, and the entire auditorium was then virtually rebuilt by Samuel Beazley. Although the semicircular brick constructional frame was retained,

the tiers were now reshaped to form a horseshoe, in the eighteenth-century Italian manner. The stage opening was widened and on each side a giant order of Corinthian columns, supporting an entablature, was built to frame the three new stage boxes – again a feature common in eighteenth- and early nineteenth-century Continental theatres.

10

Thereafter, Drury Lane was redecorated every few years to bring it into line with the mood of changing fashion. The engraving from the *Illustrated London News* of the Great Protectionist Demonstration in 1851 (*10*) shows how it looked after the redecoration of 1847, when each tier was given a bulbous front and 'laced over with a trellis of large mesh' festooned with gilt flowers. They also 'entwined' the Corinthian columns flanking the boxes. The great gas 'chandelier of gilt metal and

glass lustres, from which projected six flags of glass lustres with the lines of the Union Jack marked on them by light', was installed at the same time.

The next major reconstruction was made in 1901 by Philip Pilditch. The old theatre was then given the opulent look of turn-of-the-century Baroque: 'The tiers were reconstructed with steel girders and concrete floors, using only a front row of pillars to support them. Two rows of seats were added to each tier, and the box parapets were brought

11

forward.' This made the house more intimate, as
can be seen in this illustration of the Russian Opera
Company taking their bow in 1913 (*11*). Finally, in
1921–2, as a last flamboyant tribute to the by now
defunct tradition of the Victorian-into-Edwardian
theatre, the auditorium of Drury Lane was again
rebuilt. Wyatt's circular walls were finally
demolished by J. Emblin Walker and Associates.
The four shallow tiers surmounted by their old
uncomfortable gallery were replaced by three
immense and steeply raked balconies, their
cantilevers constructed of steel and reinforced
concrete. The new decorations were intended to echo
the late Georgian of the foyers, but they are in fact
in the stiff and uncompromising manner of the
Roman style with which Edwardian theatre
architecture ended its days (*12*).

During the lifetime of the fourth Theatre Royal,
Drury Lane, the Victorian theatre building
blossomed, flourished and died. Grafting
Continental borrowings onto native stock, the plant
flowered delicately in the self-confident climate of
mid-Victorian industrialism; exuberantly, with a
neo-Baroque flourish, in the affluence and assurance
of the *fin de siècle*; only to die finally in the
aftermath of the magnificent splendour that
characterized Edwardian imperial pomp.
Throughout the period, foreign influences were
absorbed and adapted to British needs and
circumstances with that fluency and ease which have
always been the hallmark of architecture in these
islands. The essence may be imported, but the
distillation is intensely local and personal – and
none the worse for that.

12

Colour plates

III

IV

Early and mid Victorian playhouses and opera houses

THE THEATRICAL MANAGER.

How's the house to-night?

Leaders of Fashion: Her Majesty's

In the early years of Queen Victoria's reign, Her Majesty's was the most fashionable theatre in London; with the addition in 1816–18 of the façades and colonnades by Nash and Repton to Novosielski's 1791 Opera House, it had become also the most imposing. Though it has been twice rebuilt since it burned down in 1867, one of the Nash colonnades remains as the Opera Arcade, behind the current theatre.

It was the most expensive theatre in Britain, with seats costing up to a guinea, or even two and a half guineas for Jenny Lind performances in the late 1840s. Full dress was obligatory in the pit and boxes. By the 1830s, most London theatres had acquired a few rows of comfortable stalls between the backless pit benches and the stage; Her Majesty's, known as the King's during George III's reign, already had one row of these by 1800, and by 1850 there were seven. Round the sides and down the middle of these stalls ran the broad aisles known as Fop's Alley, where the fashionable young paraded their elegance. (13) and (14) show the opening night of the opera season in March 1844. The pit boxes are smaller than usual: the seats arranged in the railway-carriage fashion popular in Italian theatres of the time, though seldom found in England.

The Italian influence, evident also in the horseshoe-shaped auditorium with its tiers of boxes,

13

14

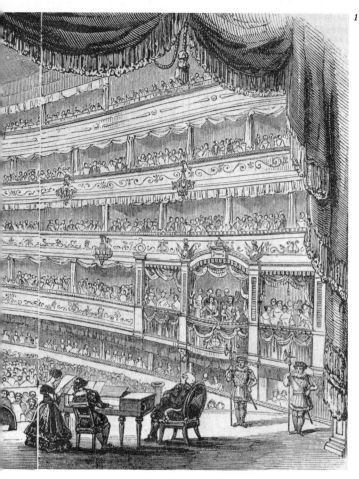

15 was appropriate since the theatre was the home of Italian opera and was generally known as the 'Italian Opera House'. The great gallery above the boxes, however, was typical of English theatres. The interior of the auditorium was frequently altered, and the division of the boxes, along with their draperies and fringes, was constantly changed. (15) shows the boxes as they appeared in 1843, at a command performance of *La figlia del'reggimento*. Gaslight was introduced in 1818, a year after Drury Lane and Covent Garden, but it was found that 'the gas imparted a deadly hue to the ladies' complexions', and in 1821 the sconces on the tier fronts were again filled with wax candles, though the central gas chandelier remained. This lighting system was retained until well into mid-century. The old deep forestage, a typical feature of seventeenth- and eighteenth-century theatres, was also retained longer at Her Majesty's than elsewhere; in fact, if these two views of different command performances are to be believed, the forestage was deeper in 1847, when the Queen came to hear Jenny Lind sing *Norma* (16), than it had been in 1843. Perhaps the presence on stage of the Beefeaters (15, extreme right) guarding Her Majesty, who was sitting above the orchestra pit, appeared somewhat incongruous. In other views of command performances, including that of 1847, they stand stolidly before the royal presence.

16

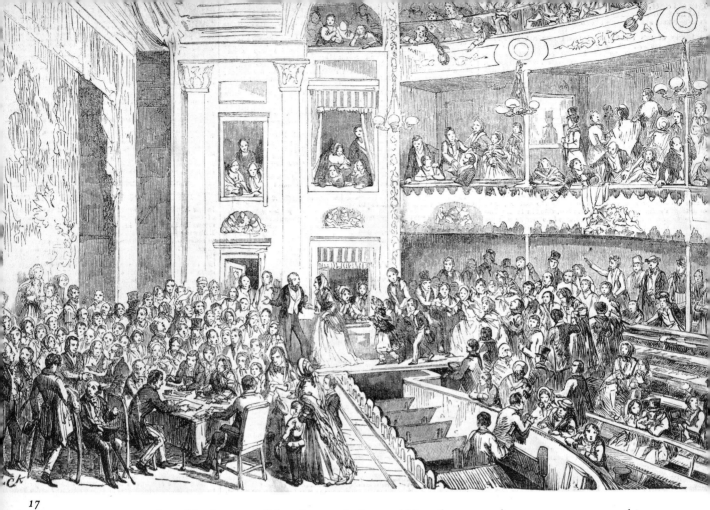

17

Adaptable theatres of the 1840s and 1850s

18

Although no new theatres were constructed in London between 1840 and 1858, the old buildings were constantly altered, redecorated or rebuilt in a variety of shapes and manners. The alterations of 1846 to Sadler's Wells (*17*) combined flat, window-like side boxes, popular earlier in the century, with semicircular open balconies which extended over the pit – an essential early-Victorian change. Both the bell-shaped Lyceum, which was redecorated in 1847 (*19*), and the Olympic, which burned down in 1849 and was rebuilt as an elongated horseshoe (*18*), have open balconies with just a few side boxes and stage boxes within a giant order. By 1856, when the Lyceum became the Royal Italian Opera, Lyceum, the old omnibus box (at stage level in the 1847 view) had disappeared (*20*); the stage was pushed back, the ceiling heightened to give greater gallery capacity, the open balconies separated into private boxes, and the gas chandeliers which emitted noxious fumes removed from the balcony fronts. A few simple changes, and a playhouse became an opera house. Planks balanced across the orchestra pit of Sadler's Wells turned it into an all-purpose hall for the Total Abstainers meeting of 1854 (*17*).

19

20

Covent Garden (1809–56)

Until 1843 only the Patent Theatres, Drury Lane
and Covent Garden, had dramatic licences, and by
the late eighteenth century these theatres had
grown so large that it was almost impossible to see
or hear the players. As a result, the actors developed
a booming, declamatory style, and the managers
produced ever more light-hearted entertainment,
attracting a somewhat mixed audience which was
given to rioting and other such pleasures of
Regency theatre-going (*21*; a Rowlandson print of
1809). With the breaking of the monopolies in
1843, however, Drury Lane and Covent Garden
lost their exclusive rights to drama, while Her
Majesty's had no longer the sole right to Italian
opera.

In 1846 it was decided to revamp the auditorium
of Covent Garden, a simple process (*22*), and
within four months a civil engineer, Benedict
Albano, had completely gutted and rebuilt the
interior to resemble La Scala (1776–8) and its
numerous Italian progeny. The theatre reopened on
6 April 1847 as the Royal Italian Opera, Covent
Garden, with Rossini's *Semiramide* (*23*) performed
in 'the presence of an immense assemblage of rank
and fashion, and of artistical and literary celebrities'.
The new company had successfully stolen Her
Majesty's audience and many of its best singers.
Enthusing after the opening night, the *Illustrated
London News* wished that 'we could add the
effect of colour, as presented on the grand
chandelier being lighted up suddenly before the
overture, an effect so electrical that it was followed
by an immense burst of cheering from all parts of
the house. The *coup d'œil* was really superb.'
The house seated over 3,000 people; even the pit,
gallery and amphitheatre benches had backs.
Albano ignored the strictures on acoustics given by
the theatrical theorists Patte and Saunders, and
used deep modelled ornament made of Canabic, a
material with a hemp basis for which he held the
patent. The theorists were proven wrong: the
house was acoustically perfect.

In carrying out his alterations, Albano changed
only Robert Smirke's auditorium of 1809 (*21*),
the foyers and the staircases. The fine façade remained
untouched, except that carriages, instead of
drawing up alongside, could now be brought
through the Greek Revival portico, thus enabling
patrons to alight under cover; surprisingly, given
the English climate, this was an innovation. The
portico was one of London's earliest examples of
the Neo-classicism so popular in France at the time.

22

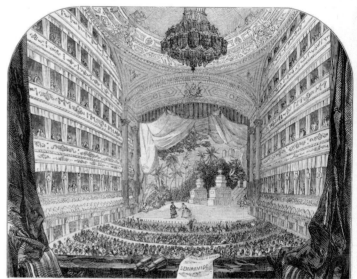

23

24

At five in the morning of 5 March 1856, at the
tag-end of a rather drunken and sleazy *bal masqué*
for which as usual the pit had been floored over,
Smirke's building burnt down (*24*). The Jeremiahs
of the day prophesied that it was the end of a
124-year-old story; there would be no more Royal
Opera House, Covent Garden.

25

26

27

28

Barry's Covent Garden (1858)

On 15 May 1858, the Royal Opera House
reopened, rebuilt from scratch (*25–8*). The
architect, E. M. Barry, had achieved the entire
operation in just six months. Although the
auditorium is more spacious than its predecessor,
and its stage larger, the building as a whole is
smaller. The previous theatre had completely
occupied the site, including the part now taken up
by the Floral Hall (1860). The circulation spaces are
cramped and less imposing than they had been
before. The old auditorium had run parallel to the
portico in Bow Street, whereas the new one is at
right angles to it. The photograph (*27*), taken
c. 1890 before the addition to the crush bar of the
glass conservatory, shows Barry's neo-Palladian
building to be a very fair copy of von
Knobelsdorff's great Staatsoper (1741–2) on Unter
den Linden, Berlin.

The oldest and quite the most beautiful
surviving Victorian theatre in Britain, the
auditorium gains its effect by its clarity of purpose
and delicacy of decoration (see colour plate 1). The
splendid saucer dome unifies the whole, adding to
the superb atmosphere of the house. The pit floor
had ten straight rows of stalls and eight rows of pit,
all removable. It was designed so that it could be
cranked up to stage level, making it possible to use
the entire area for the great balls and receptions that
were a feature of the period.

29

Covent Garden Galas

Since its opening in 1858 the Garden has been
recognized as the most important State theatre of
the country, eclipsing Drury Lane and completely
outshining Her Majesty's, which never regained its
former reputation. Great galas at the Royal Opera
House have always been an essential part of State
visits to Britain. On such occasions, the royal party
is accommodated in the centre of the grand tier,
rather than in the royal box to the right of the
stage which has its own private retiring-room
behind and a separate entrance in Floral Street.

(*29*) shows the visit of the German Emperor and
Empress in 1891. The convention that ladies sitting
in the boxes should carry a bouquet of flowers to
the theatre seems to have come into existence in the
1860s and continued until the turn of the century.
Fans were not only decorative and becoming but
also a necessity in the badly ventilated house.

(*30*) is a gala in 1969 to commemorate Dame
Margot Fonteyn's 35 years' association with the
Royal Ballet. The photograph was taken from the
circular apex to the dome, an aperture which
formerly ventilated the great gas chandelier,
removed *c.* 1900 when complete conversion from
gas to electricity took place. Electricity had already
been fitted to the sconces on the tier fronts in
1892. The removal of the chandelier greatly
improved the sightlines from the amphitheatre
and gallery, which were reraked, reseated and
combined into one unit in 1964.

30

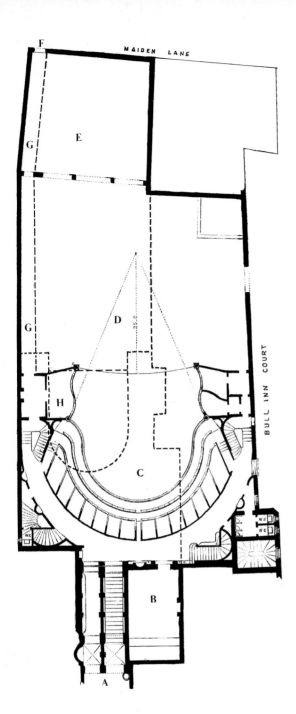

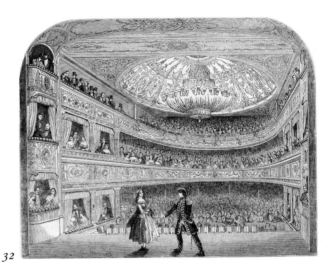

32

31 THE ADELPHI

Plan in 1858

A Entrance from Strand
B Saloon
C Auditorium
D Stage
E Dressing rooms etc.
F Queen's entrance in
   Maiden Lane
G Corridor to Queen's box
H Queen's box and saloon

The dotted line shows the
extent of the former theatre

33 Left. The Strand frontage in
the 1840s

The new sophistication: the Adelphi (1858)

Despite its beauty, Covent Garden was in some
ways very conservative; the Theatre Royal,
Adelphi, also completed in 1858 (*34*), had a far
more complicated and sophisticated architectural
solution. The sinuosity of T. H. Wyatt's plan (*31*)
and grand tier *balcon* cantilevering six feet out from
the balcony columns was made possible by 'the
application of iron in modes which are altering the
structural character of this class of building'
(*The Builder*, 11 December 1858). The wrought-iron
roof trusses, riveted in parts, were carried on
stanchions which continued right down to the
foundations, so that the entire ceiling was hung;
even the box fronts were braced by 'girders bent to
the forms of the boxes'. The projecting *balcon*,
backed by semi-private boxes, was typical of
French architecture. In the Romantic period it had
been customary for ladies *en grande toilette* to fill the
boxes completely, while their escorts stood or sat
behind. At the Adelphi, the front of the *balcon* was
of open work so that the ladies' dresses could be
seen.

Seating created a new standard of comfort; the
orchestra stalls were 24 inches centre to centre and
16 inches deep, as against the 21 by 15 inches of the
Olympic (*18*). Altogether, the Adelphi was far
grander and more spacious than any other
commercial theatre in London. The proscenium
opening was 35 feet wide and 38 feet high, in contrast
to the Lyceum's 32 by 35 feet (*20*) and the Olympic's
27 by 29 feet. As a result, the sightlines from all
parts of the house were much improved.

34

35

A comparison with the old Adelphi, as reconstructed and redecorated in 1846 (*31*; the dotted lines on plan), shows dramatically how the wealth of the Industrial Revolution was altering the character of the minor theatres of London. The suave professionalism of the new building contrasts sharply with the almost amateur quality of the old (*32*), although the theatre was still well back from the main street, the Strand, and was approached down a series of corridors and poky halls (*31, 35*); land values on main thoroughfares were far too high to be wasted on theatres. To reach the royal box and anteroom, the Queen was obliged to proceed along a 90-foot corridor from her private entrance in Maiden Lane.

36

1850s into 1860s

The boom in theatre building dates from about 1858. Increasing prosperity, easier travelling conditions and a steadily growing population began to turn the clamour for entertainment into a roar and, by the 1900s, Britain was filled with thousands of theatres. Though the nineteenth century seems in retrospect to be one of unity and stability, each decade produced its own style of theatre architecture. Some theatres looked backward, others forward; but all, despite their variety, now appear typical of their own particular time.

The Royal Pavilion Theatre, Whitechapel Road (1858; *36*), designed by G. H. Simmonds, was known as the Drury Lane of the East, probably because the giant order containing three stage boxes overlooking the forestage was reminiscent of Beazley's 1822 reconstruction of Drury Lane. The magnificent auditorium was designed to hold

3,000 people; the majority of the audience was poor, and hence its immense gallery with cheaply-priced seats. Although the engraving belies the fact, the pit is said to have accommodated 2,000 people. The theatre looks backward architecturally; the boxes surround the pit, whereas the pit extended quite deeply under the first balcony in the Adelphi, built in the same year, and also in the Holborn Theatre (*37*), designed in 1866 by Finch, Hill and Paraire for the theatrical entrepreneur and speculator Sefton Parry. By the mid-1860s, open balconies projecting well over the pit had become usual practice, and the forestage had completely disappeared. Ventilation was improved, with openings in 'the most convenient positions to avoid draughts, while the heated atmosphere is allowed to escape into the roof by perforations in the ceiling'. The Holborn was a small commercial London

37

38

theatre, built very much on the cheap and in the simplest possible way; it was designed to hold 1,500 people who were squeezed in tight. There were no aisles. Sefton Parry had spent some years barnstorming in the Cape of Good Hope, and was always out to make a quick profit. Later, he was said to have built the Avenue Theatre with the express intention of getting it requisitioned by the South-Eastern Railway. Few theatres of the 1860s survive. The Royal Marylebone, off the Edgware Road, had once boasted the deepest stage in London and had enjoyed the patronage of royalty. Blitzed during the war, it ended its days as the storeroom of a junk merchant. The photograph (38), taken in the mid-1950s not long before the theatre's final demolition, gives some idea of the spatial qualities enjoyed by a minor theatre of the period.

39

West End commercialism: the Globe (1868)

Another of Sefton Parry's 'spec' theatres, this time
designed by himself, the Globe in Newcastle
Street, Strand, was hastily and shoddily built but
was nevertheless eminently neat and practical;
it had a delightful atmosphere and excellent
sightlines and acoustics (39). The dome and balcony
fronts were completely circular in plan, and for the
first time the dress circle and private boxes were at
street level, a practice which later became general
in West End theatres. The 'best' patrons walked
straight in, while the stalls and pit customers
descended 12 feet to their seats and the
amphitheatre and gallery people climbed up. There
were only 130 dress-circle seats and six boxes at the
most convenient level, with 90 orchestra stalls and
560 pit places below; above were 130 amphitheatre
seats and bench-space for 600 in the gallery.
Nevertheless, the audience had considerably fewer
stairs to climb than in other theatres at the
time.

The Globe presented a very mean face to the
street, as did its sister theatre, the Opéra Comique
(1870), which was built back-to-back with the
Globe and was approached from the Strand
through a subterranean alley under Holywell
Street. These two little theatres were known as the
Rickety Twins but, despite their name, neither
collapsed nor burned down. The owners had hoped
that the entire area would be redeveloped so that
they would receive good compensation, but this
did not come about until the turn of the century
when the area was cleared to make way for the
creation of Aldwych and Kingsway. The
photograph (40) was taken shortly before the
theatre was demolished in 1902.

The provinces in the 1860s

By the 1850s, all the major railway networks of Britain had been completed, and as a result the old 'theatre circuit' companies, which had confined themselves to one region, were gradually replaced by London artists who could now tour with speed and in comfort. Commercial theatres in the provinces were if anything grander than their metropolitan prototypes, having more the character of civic theatres; some even offered entrance under cover for carriages. In the Prince of Wales's, Liverpool (43), built in 1866, a carriage-way ran under the outer left-hand arch, thus facilitating the entry of those who arrived in modest carriages or cabs; the very rich, like the heroine of the satire *Miss Kilmansegg and her Precious Leg*, had their own coachmen and umbrella-bearing footmen (41).

The Prince's, Manchester (*c.* 1864; 42), like the Prince of Wales's, was designed by Edward Salomons of Manchester and Liverpool. He also designed Manchester's Free Trade Hall, of which the name and function were very apposite to the period.

Besides the carriage-way, the Italianate façade of the Prince of Wales's is interesting in that its arches contain, not only pedestrian entrances to the stalls and boxes (43 centre) and the pit circle (43 far right), but also two shops, one of which led to extensive supper-rooms. The lions' heads above the lamps on the pilasters were in fact ventilation apertures. The architect was at pains to provide better ventilation than hitherto by using an elaborate system of air shafts converging above the central chandelier. Even the complicated stage machinery was much improved; it was now driven by an engine and a boiler, situated on a level below the understage machinery-floor. The old system of visible footlights (42) was replaced by an enamelled-iron box-trough set into the stage floor, a novelty which subsequently became the norm.

41

42

43

Theatre Royal Nottingham.

44

The 1860s saw the emergence of the specialist theatre architect, who was London-based and designed theatres all over Britain. The first, and one of the greatest, was C. J. Phipps (1835–97), whose extant Theatre Royal, Nottingham, of 1865 (*44*) is an elegant crib of the Parisian Théâtre Italien, the Salle Favart (1781–3), and the many Neo-classic copies of it built in France during the first decades of the nineteenth century.

The rise of the music hall

The phenomenal vitality of the Victorian music hall, which became formalized when it moved into buildings that did it justice, originated in the tavern, where entertainment naturally included food and drink. Although it is difficult to date its beginnings, among its antecedents were the pleasure-gardens of the eighteenth century and the Comus Courts in the taverns: the latter being farcical mock trials and satirical jibes at pompous and prominent people. The judge in these mock trials later became the chairman in the music hall.

Before 1843 the taverns had vied with the minor theatres in presenting very similar fare: serious entertainment interspersed to various degrees with songs and dances. But in freeing the minor theatres from performing dramatic work with a musical accompaniment, the 1843 Act (see Introduction, p. 8) also prohibited dramatic entertainment accompanied by eating and drinking in the auditorium. The saloon theatres, the taverns seeking to entertain their paying customers, like the famous Grecian in the City Road (see pp. 52–3), had to confine themselves to music hall proper – often anything but proper. By the 1850s dozens of taverns had built long-rooms with a stage at one end, like the music hall in Evan's Hotel, Covent Garden (1857; 45); or with a balcony above for non-drinking customers, as in the Lord Nelson Tavern, St Pancras, licensed for entertainment from 1852 but depicted here in 1856 (46). Evan's, with its all-male, top-hatted clientele, had the atmosphere of a gentlemen's club, while the Argyll Rooms, as seen here in 1863 (47), were not the kind of ambience to which a gentleman submitted his wife.

These infamous Rooms later gained respectability, after the rebuilding in 1882, as the Royal Trocadero Palace of Varieties, and after 1902 as the famous Trocadero Restaurant, now refurbished as a gambling casino, discotheque and bowling alley called Tiffany's. This progression from pub music hall into Palace of Varieties was typical; churches, concert halls and places of 'artistic and scientific edification' were also taken over for similar purposes. In their heyday, from 1880 to 1910, hundreds of music halls were built all over the country, far outnumbering the straight theatres constructed during the same period. Indeed, many of these theatres and even opera houses soon became music halls.

THE LORD NELSON TAVERN.

46

47

Music halls: the concert hall influence

Architecturally, music halls borrowed from many traditions; besides being influenced by the tavern long-room and the theatre, they also took over elements from the concert hall, which was already well established by the mid-century. For example, the small Concert Room of St George's Hall, Liverpool (48), designed by Harvey Lonsdale Elmes in 1836 and completed in 1847 by C. R. Cockerell, has certain features of ornament and form which became common in later music halls. The straight-sided and balconied Philharmonic Hall, Liverpool (1846–9; 49), by John Cunningham, with its uncurtained stage at one end, could be any one of many similar buildings built as music halls from the 1860s to the early 1890s, such as McDonald's (1864; 52, 53), or Newcastle's Empire (1891; 113–18). The somewhat flat, rectangular and balconied appearance is atypical of other theatre architecture of the period; particularly like it, however, in shape, function and character was the concert hall (1856) in the Surrey Zoological Gardens, Southwark, designed by Horace Jones and known as the Music Hall (50, 51). It was erected in four months, and had a seating capacity of 10,000, with room for 1,000 musicians. Performances of all kinds of music took place there, in particular the famous concerts of M. Jullien. Stylistically it was most eclectic, 'degenerate Italian, with a large infusion of French taste'. The staircase towers were topped with Turkish kiosks; a zinc-roofed upper storey suggested Palladio's Basilica at Vicenza; and the entire conglomeration heralded the marvellous architecture of entertainment which made the music halls such fun.

50, 51

McDonald's Music Hall (1864)

McDonald's Music Hall, Hoxton (1864; *52, 53*), is Surrey Gardens Hall in miniature: a pub long-room in scale, but built specifically for variety entertainment. Even the bulbous cast-iron balcony fronts echo Surrey Gardens. Licensed from 1864 to 1871 as a music hall and listed as such in the Shoreditch ratebooks from 1877 to 1883, McDonald's still survives as a Friends' Neighbourhood Centre. The photographs, taken at the centenary celebrations of an 'old-time' music hall performance in 1963, give some idea of the convivial intimacy enjoyed by the boisterous popular audiences who once crowded it.

Buildings like McDonald's were particularly cheap to erect. Components were already mass-produced by this time, and cast-iron columns, ornamental capitals, decorative railings and galvanized-iron roofing were readily available from the catalogues of the builders' merchants. *The Builder*, reviewing the Music Hall in Surrey Gardens in 1856, complains that 'the chandeliers, brought in a hurry from the glass warehouse, should be exchanged for something from the architect's own design', and that 'full consideration of details by an architect himself is impossible under the present system of executing works'. A jibe at builders in a hurry – one of the very merits of Victorian efficiency. The immense Surrey Gardens Hall cost only £18,200, and in that same year a stalls seat at the Queen's Concert Rooms, Hanover Square, cost ten shillings and sixpence – an indication of how quickly the cost of the building would be recovered.

52

53

54

55

56

Triumph of frivolity over virtue: the Alhambra (1851 *et seq.*)

The Alhambra is the best example of a building originally created as a place of 'artistic and scientific edification' but soon taken over by the music hall, which thus made its own an architectural style intended for higher things. Conceived in 1850, the year before the Great Exhibition, as the Royal Panopticon of Science and Art, the building appeared in the *Illustrated London News* of 31 January 1852 in all its Saracenic glory, 'a style which has as yet no perfect exemplification in the metropolis'. The great onion dome, which was never realized, was copied by the architect T. Hayter Lewis from a daguerreotype of a mosque in Cairo (54).

The Victorians were thoroughly bored by what they considered to be the monotonous, stereotyped architecture of Georgian England, which they found uninformed and parochial, even vulgar. They wanted something far more colourful, an attitude shared by many people today after decades of the Modern Movement. When the Panopticon opened on 18 March 1854 the façade, save for minor changes, was that of the first design, but with the original dome replaced by a low sixteen-sided cone. Inside (55), a rotunda 97 feet in diameter and in height held two main galleries facing an immense organ, set into its own double-bayed, proscenium-like recess (not shown). Various engineering machines, the wonders of the age, were exhibited among copies of well-known statues. To the right of the one on the ground floor, behind the fountain, can be seen a strange bird-cage structure, surmounted by a pole. This was an 'Ascending Carriage' which elevated sightseers up to the galleries. Worked hydraulically, this passenger lift was one of the earliest to be installed in a public place, anywhere.

But the Panopticon was not a success; apparently the committee of clerics and businessmen who ran it could not agree. The high-minded Moorish folly was sold up and on 3 April 1858, with E. T. Smith as its new owner, it opened as the Alhambra Palace with Howes and Cushing's American circus. The central fountain gave way to a circus ring; the great organ was sold to St Paul's Cathedral, and Queen Victoria, who had ignored the building in its serious guise, brought her children to the circus. (57) shows her in 1855 passing through Leicester Square with Louis Napoléon and the Empress Eugénie, *en route* to the Opera. The Panopticon is alight and festive, while Wyld's Great Globe glows darkly behind the royal carriage.

In October 1858, Smith obtained a licence for music and dancing. In 1860 he erected a proscenium frame around the old organ recess, furnished the floor with tables and chairs and renamed it the Royal Alhambra Palace Music Hall (56). Those who went to the first night gasped in admiration at the more-Moorish-than-ever redecoration: the house was set on its giddy, exotic way. Certainly, there were difficulties. Drinking, dancing and merriment were never viewed favourably by the police and excuses were found for harassment and closure. The tables and chairs were removed in 1871 and the pit was reseated like a normal theatre. The bars, the cause of all the trouble, had formerly commanded a view of the stage; they were 'now to be found in snug nooks and sly corners'.

5

In 1881, the Alhambra was embellished with an enlarged proscenium and with boxes inserted between the balconies. It was then fitted with stepped rows of seats. On the night of 7 September 1882, fire destroyed everything but the front wall and the internal columns with their pointed horseshoe arches. It was decided to rebuild immediately in the same style but with fireproof materials, and the building reopened on 3 December 1883 (58). By then, the Saracenic medley of the Panopticon had come to be known as Alhambresque. Further partial reconstruction was carried out in 1888, 1892, 1897, 1907 and 1912.

(59) shows the special performance of the *Entente Cordiale* ballet given in 1905 to celebrate the new alliance between England and France. The Alhambra was finally demolished in 1936 and the Odeon Cinema erected on the site.

58

59

Disreputable music halls in the 1870s

ALLY AT THE ELEPHANT AND CASTLE.

"The majority of well-regulated people, if asked to express an opinion, would say that Poor Papa is, to all intents and purposes, an imbecile—he does such extraordinary things. His latest move is to secure a private box for the run of "Jack the Giant Killer" at the Elephant and Castle Theatre, and every night some members of the Family honour the performance with a visit. The other evening the conductor was unable to fulfil his duties, and Mr. Burton Green asked Papa to kindly take his place. The overture was a big success; but the conduct of some of the younger members of the Family was most unbecoming."—TOOTSIE.

60

Music halls flourished in the poorer areas, but they were neither sanitary nor safe and despite their charm they were certainly uncomfortable.

The Colosseum, Liverpool, converted from an old Unitarian chapel around 1850 and subsequently modernized, was the scene in 1878 (*61*) of one of the many disasters of pre-regulation days. A portion of the ceiling fell, there was a false alarm of fire and 37 people were killed in the ensuing panic.

When the Grecian, Shoreditch, was rebuilt for the last time in 1876–7 (*62* centre), it was the end of an era during which the site had fused three elements of entertainment: a pleasure garden (*62* top left), a theatre, and a variety saloon called the Eagle. When it was bought by General Booth for the Salvation Army in 1882, this fusion had become an anachronism; since 1870 the premises had been disreputable and they were a suitable capture for the Hallelujah Lads and Lasses, who appear to be enjoying themselves – like Ally Sloper at the Elephant and Castle (1878; *60*), Frank Matcham's first theatre.

61

PAY HERE.
RESERVED SEATS 2/-
BOXES 1/-

WHERE THE DISASTER OCCURRED

PRINCIPAL ENTRANCE

62

1. In the Grounds. —2. A Duet by the Misses Booth. —3. The Afternoon Meeting in the Grecian Theatre. —4. A Band of Hallelujah Lasses. —5. The General and Mrs. Booth.

THE SALVATION ARMY—"THE CAPTURE OF THE EAGLE"

Music halls of the slums in the 1880s

*. . . there are two houses nightly. From seven till nine
dramas are performed, then everybody is turned out and
the house is refilled . . . for a music-hall entertainment –
and nearly every evening the theatre is crammed to
suffocation; the admission is 1d the gallery, 2d the pit,
and 3d and 6d the upper circle and boxes. On the night
of our visit there wasn't room to cram another boy in the
place; the gallery and pit were full of boys and girls of
from eight to fifteen . . . and the bulk of the audience in
the other parts were quite young people. . . . It was a
jam – not a crowd – when one boy coughed it shook the
thousands wedged in and round about; and when one
boy got up to go out he had to crawl and walk over the
heads of the others. . . .*

*The entertainment was admirable; the artists were
clever, and in only one case absolutely vulgar; and the
choruses were joined in by the entire assembled
multitude. . . .*

*Of course there are disturbances, but the remedy is
short and effective. Two young gentlemen in the dress
circle fought and used bad language to each other.
Quick as lightning the official was upstairs with a
solitary policeman, the delinquents were seized by the
collar, and, before they could expostulate, flung down a
flight of steps and hustled out into the street with a
celerity which could only come of constant practice.*

George R. Sims in *Ally Sloper's Half-Holiday*,
21 January 1888 (63).

63

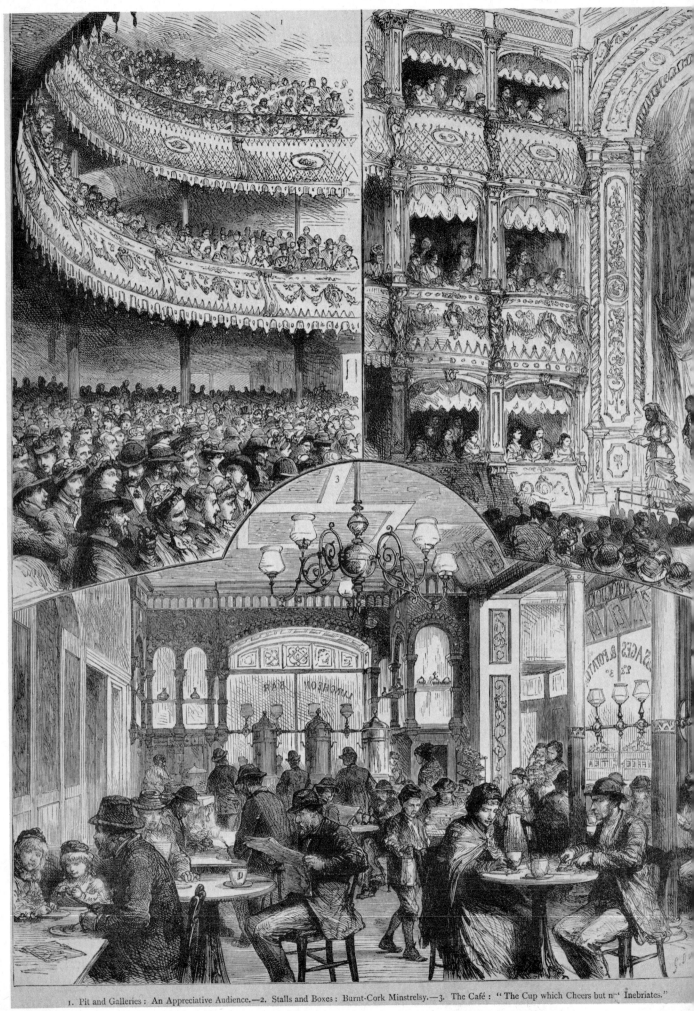

1. Pit and Galleries: An Appreciative Audience. — 2. Stalls and Boxes: Burnt-Cork Minstrelsy. — 3. The Café: "The Cup which Cheers but not Inebriates."

Music halls: social and technical improvements of the 1880s

The fortunes of the famous Old Vic had been declining steadily and despite the extensive alterations to the auditorium of 1871 (*64* top) the place had become a 'sink of iniquity'. Emma Cons took it over in 1880 and renamed it the Royal Victoria Hall and Coffee Tavern (*64* bottom). Fortunately the interior, with its tight, bulging side boxes, typical of the 1870s (see also *62*), was left intact. The boxes have since been swallowed up by the stage, but the balcony fronts survive.

Overcrowding and gas fumes in the theatres of the 1880s were appalling. A Dr Angus Smith reported in 1884 that the air in the dress circles of most theatres was found on analysis to be fouler than that taken from a sewer. Audiences eager for fresh air poured into the draughty corridors during the intervals (*65*). Throughout the century architects had tried to improve these conditions, but Frank Matcham (1854–1920) offered the most successful solutions. In the Paragon Theatre of Varieties, Mile End Road (1884–5; *66*), he placed the air-intake vents six feet above ground level, thus eliminating draughts, and also created a better extract system above the 'sun-burner' (the central chandelier, not shown in the cross-section). The Paragon was advertised as the 'Best ventilated theatre in London'. It made Matcham's reputation and he subsequently designed some 200 other theatres.

65   WHEN AIR IS NECESSARY.

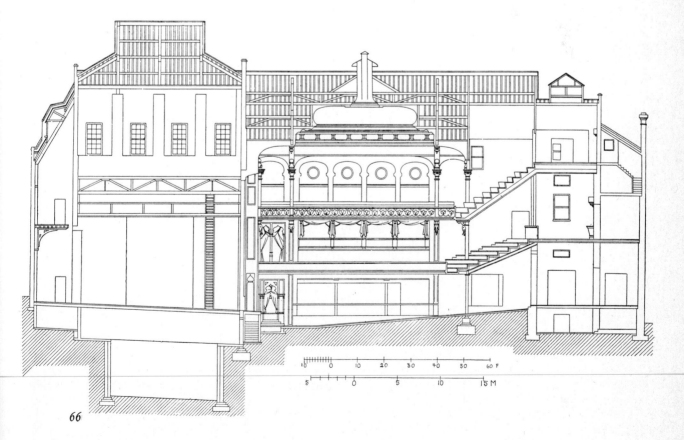

66

Late Victorian and Edwardian Theatres: changes and innovations after 1870

The social and economic forces which stimulated the boom in theatre-building generated a greater awareness of the theatre as a civic amenity. The British theatre, always a commercial venture, was from a design point of view a poor relative of the opulent, subsidized state and civic theatres of the Continent, though these did have some influence on style and civic attitudes in Britain. Although never monumental (except for the unique Shakespeare Memorial), the theatre was given more serious design consideration, particularly where commissions were gained from architectural competitions. Foreign styles became increasingly prevalent: French Empire, Viennese Baroque, Bavarian Rococo; some theatre exteriors were even designed in a modified Gothic style which, in the 'Battle of the Styles', had become the accepted norm for church architecture as the Classic style was for public buildings. (67) shows the mixture of French, German and Venetian Romanesque used on the façade of the Leeds Grand (see also 72–5 and colour plate II).

The music hall, in its own supremely eccentric way, combined everything: Baroque, Oriental, Gothic, Flemish, Middle Eastern – the entire cornucopia of architectural history. Buildings designed specifically as theatres or opera houses were more sober, though even their architecture became increasingly florid. By the 'nineties, the increasing interchange of function blurred the frontiers between theatre and music hall, each finally taking on the characteristics of the other. Often it is only the distinctive lunette on either side of the proscenium frame, indicating the programme number of the variety act, which clearly tells us 'music hall'.

A number of disastrous fires in many theatres finally led to legislation (Sachs, in his prodigious *Modern Opera Houses and Theatres*, published in 1896–8, calculated that the average life of a theatre was twelve years). After 1878, a proliferation of regulations controlled, not only entrance and egress, doors, staircases, seating capacities, stages, equipment, etc., but also the choice of site. One clause which prescribed that 'at least half the boundary of the theatre should abut on a public highway' resulted in the corner siting which became usual after the 'nineties. Theatres could no longer be cramped into the most profitable but least safe places.

From the early 1880s, greater technical prowess led to many changes. Electric light was first introduced in the Savoy in 1881; with subsequent refinements, it gradually replaced the foul-smelling, oxygen-consuming gas burners. In order to increase seating capacity without placing the expensive dress-circle seats too far from the stage, an abortive attempt was made at the Haymarket, in the previous year, to eliminate the pit which had been crawling ever deeper under the dress circle. Similarly, balconies were growing steadily deeper, but had to be supported by columns which obstructed sightlines. During the 1880s and particularly in the early 1890s, with the development of steel construction, deep cantilevered balconies became possible and the columns were made redundant.

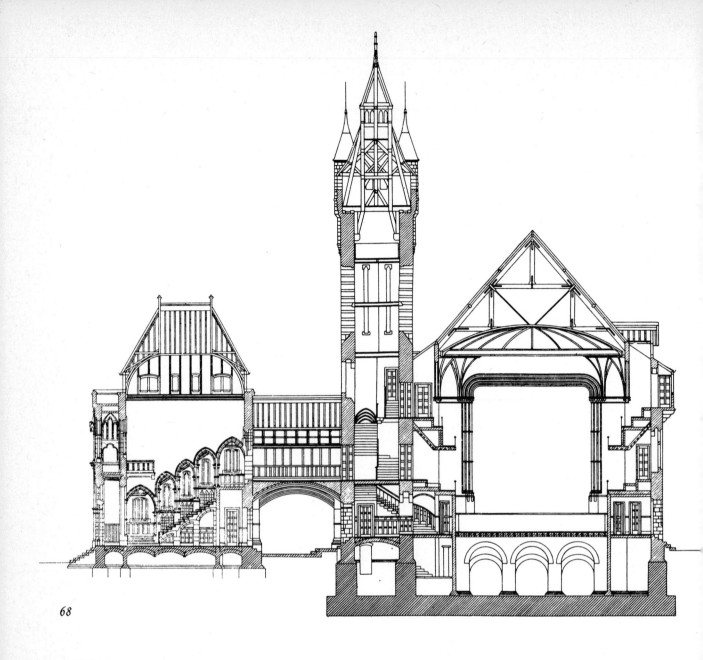

68

Gothicizing:
the Shakespeare Memorial (1877–79)

On the tercentenary of Shakespeare's birth it was
decided to build a monument at Stratford-upon-
Avon. Argument as to what form it should take
held up the project for ten years, but finally it was
agreed that there should be a theatre and museum,
and the competition to choose the design was won
by Dodgshun and Unsworth. In April 1877 the
foundation stone was laid, and the theatre opened
on 23 April 1879, with Helen Faucit and Barry
Sullivan in *Much Ado About Nothing* (71). To lessen
the fire risk, a gallery separated the museum from
the theatre. Patrons sitting in the two tiers entered
via the museum and this gallery, while the stalls
were approached from underneath it (68).

The entire beautifully balanced ensemble was
carried out in a romantic and graceful mixture of
Gothic and Tudor (69). Highly unusual for an

English theatre at the time, as Sachs remarked in
1897, was 'the way in which the structure
expresses its purpose on the exterior . . . fully in
accordance with the most recent ideas on that
point'. The tower was entirely ornamental and, like
the museum, was not completed until some years
later. Internally, a circular screen of Gothic arches
carried the auditorium ceiling (70); the narrow
proscenium arch, flanked by clustered piers, had a
Tudor look about it (71). The building cost
£20,000, and nearly £11,500 of this was spent on
the theatre itself, which seated 900. Unfortunately,
this delightful building was destroyed by fire in
March 1926, although the museum block and
bridge remained unscathed. The shell of the old
auditorium was adapted into a conference room
when the new theatre was built in 1929–32.

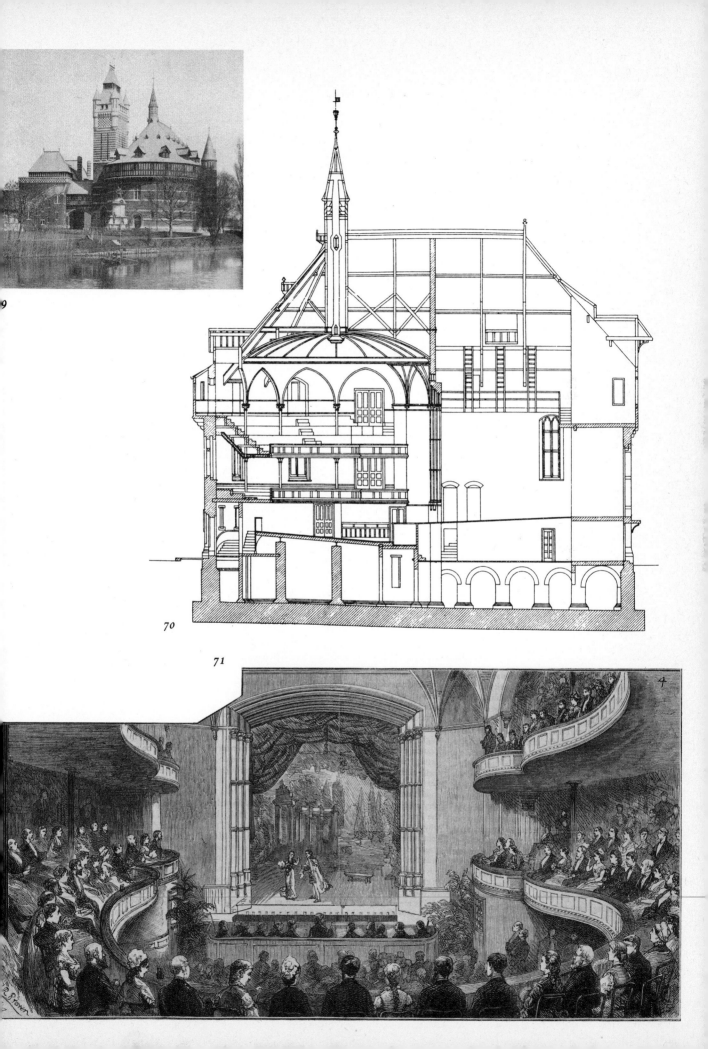

69

70

71

4

Gothicizing: the Grand, Leeds (1878)

Another example of an eclectic neo-Gothic style is the superb Leeds Grand Theatre and Opera House (1878), still one of the finest theatres in Britain. By the mid-century, the major industrial cities had developed their own individual character. The prosperous textile, engineering and ready-made clothing manufacturers of Leeds had expressed their individuality in Cuthbert Brodrick's grandiose Town Hall (1853–8) and Corn Exchange (1860). The Grand Theatre, designed by George Carson, expressed a similar attitude of civic pride, and the fascinating and sensible arcades of the last decades of the nineteenth century gave tangible evidence of an individuality still evident in the third quarter of the twentieth.

The Grand was in effect a cultural and shopping centre (see plan 72). Beneath the concert hall, now a cinema, was a series of six shops; the main entrance to the theatre was under the grand saloon and like the concert hall it ran parallel with the main street, New Briggate. The theatre was contained, as a protection against fire, in a quite separate structure. Fire precaution was, for that time, most carefully considered; the architect allowed for each unit of the building to be closed off independently in case of emergency. The stage facilities are all accessible from a side street. In the 1870s, touring companies expected to have scenery and props provided for them on arrival, and as a result there are scene shops, rehearsal rooms, and a paint frame in its own paint shop *behind* the stage, unlike the standard cramped practice of using the back wall of the stage. The theatre had its own gas-making plant, and even a pottery for firing props and utensils.

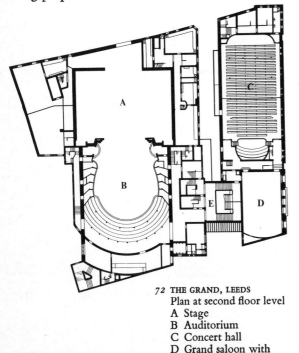

72 THE GRAND, LEEDS
Plan at second floor level
A Stage
B Auditorium
C Concert hall
D Grand saloon with main entrance under
E Main staircase

This skilful planning is reflected in the richly decorated auditorium. Although a large house (it originally accommodated 3,200, with 2,600 seated and 600 standing, and now seats 1,552 with 100 standing), the sense of intimacy is remarkable, and the atmosphere exciting and highly theatrical. Three relatively shallow tiers are stacked as tightly as possible (74), each successive tier dipping down from its centre and set back from the one below it (73). This dipping line is carried on by the side boxes, the seats of which are also forward of those in the boxes above. The horns of the box tiers are finally rounded off. This careful planning, both in section and in plan, produces a perfect sightline from almost every seat, a technical achievement unusual in British theatres.

The decoration of the theatre was handled with comparable *bravura*. Four fretted fan vaults seemingly support a shallow saucer dome, enriched with deep modelled ornament of Second Empire flamboyance. The clustered piers flanking the proscenium arch provide another Gothic touch (75), while the deep undercutting of the plasterwork on the tier fronts has the ebullience of a Corinthian frieze. The royal boxes are set within a Cinquecento frame; unfortunately, the giant goddesses which once adorned them have been removed and are now stored, undamaged, in the old pottery. Otherwise, the house still preserves intact its 1870s bombast, worthy of a grand theatre in Brussels, Paris or Vienna.

(See also colour plate II.)

75

Thomas Verity and French influence

Verity was one of the first English architects to design in an authentic French manner. His Criterion (1870–3), a commission he won in competition, had a magnificent, expensively built French Renaissance façade typical of Second Empire Paris (76). The entire conception of a restaurant and theatre built completely underground heralded a new era of pomp and good living. However, in practical terms the theatre was stuffy and cramped, despite the air pumped down into it; it was rebuilt in 1884 and since then has remained basically intact (81–4, overleaf). The photograph (76) was taken between 1876 and 1880, when the addition to the original building was constructed and before the creation of Piccadilly Circus in 1885.

By 1884 Verity had completed the Comedy (1881; 77) and the Empire (1882–4; 78–80). The photograph (79), taken in 1915, shows what happens to a theatre when the architects do not make provision for advertising: the unit formed by the neat pediment and the pilasters framing the great central window, a feature used on the *piano nobile* of the Criterion, is defaced by the inevitable poster.

The opening of the Empire was delayed by 'the very positive demands of the Board of Works', which was newly aware of fire hazards. As a result, the theatre was equipped with better entrances and exits, while the tiers and corridors were constructed of fireproof materials. A special and novel feature was the '*foyer*, which was so generally popular on the Continent' (80, top left). A spacious staircase (80, bottom left) provided access to the foyer and to the two promenades surrounding the tiers which were later to become notorious as the haunt of prostitutes (80, top right, and 78).

76

77

AT THE "EMPIRE."

78

79

80

The Criterion   Drawings made of the Criterion in 1884 show that
the theatre has hardly altered at all, despite some
remodelling and redecoration in 1902–3. The tiny
foyer fronting on Piccadilly Circus is cunningly
given an air of spaciousness by the juxtaposition of
mirrors, painted ceiling panels, and the famous and
witty coloured tiling (*82, 83*). The tiling also lines
the staircase (*84*) leading down to the subterranean
auditorium, which seats 660 on three levels: stalls,
dress circle and upper circle. The house is
delightfully alive and intimate, as can be seen from
this photograph (*81*) taken from behind the back
row of the dress circle. When repainting some years
ago, the management wisely chose the soft muted
colours and delicate gilding typical of the early
1880s. Intense deep reds and opulent heavy gold
were not fashionable in the West End until the
following decade.

81

82

83

84

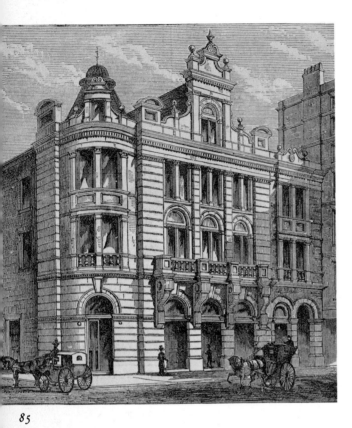

85

86

Electric light at the Savoy (1881)

The great theatrical event of 1881 was the opening
of the Savoy Theatre (*85*) with Gilbert and
Sullivan's *Patience*. D'Oyly Carte knew exactly
what he wanted from Phipps, the designer. For the
first time anywhere in the world, a public building
was lit entirely with 'the electric light', supplied by
Messrs Siemens Brothers and made possible by 'the
incandescent lamps of Mr J. W. Swan of
Newcastle-on-Tyne', which were 'experimentally
applied to the interior of this theatre'; gas was still
there in case of emergency. This experiment was to
revolutionize, not only theatre lighting, but also
women's jewellery; diamonds sparkled so much
more efficiently that coloured stones went out of
fashion. Make-up had to be softened too, for some
grandes dames appeared under electric light to be
painted up like Jezebels.

Full evening dress was of course still compulsory
for stalls, box and dress circle patrons. (*86*) shows
them leaving Irving's Lyceum in 1881. Beazley's
portico (1834), like that of Nash's Haymarket, has
survived the various rebuildings of the auditorium.
In Irving's day, the interior was basically that of
1856 (*20*).

87

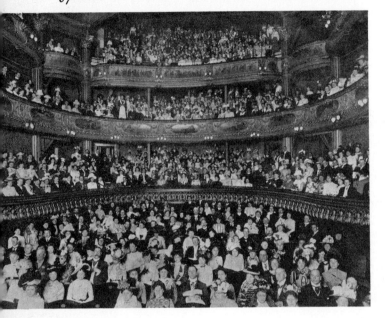

88

Pit: abolition and 'pittites'

Nash's famous Haymarket (1821; *87*) had been altered several times before it was taken over by the Bancrofts in 1879. Phipps, the most prominent theatre architect in Britain at that time, tried to recreate the interior of Victor Louis's Grand Théâtre de Bordeaux (1773–80), and in the process abolished the pit under the first balcony and seated the entire area below the dress circle with expensive stalls seats (*88*); the theatre is also important in being the first to have a complete four-sided picture-frame for its proscenium. 'Pittites' were given an upper balcony, which did not please them, and the result was a minor riot on the opening night. The experiment does not appear to have been repeated elsewhere; instead, pits grew deeper and deeper, and when the Haymarket was again rebuilt in 1904 the pit was brought back.

'Pittites' were a special breed. The text from *The Graphic* of 17 January 1891, with drawings by Hugh Thomson (*89–92*), considers that 'some poet ought to sing the praises of this dauntless band! . . . Great, no doubt – upon occasion – is the enthusiasm of gallery and upper circle, and also of stalls, when they are manned by "mashers". But the pittites are the most faithful as well as the most fervid of the play-going classes. Nothing deters them – not even the terrors of a tropical afternoon or the horrors of an arctic night. They remain true to their favourite play, player or playhouse.' Their fanaticism was demonstrated by 'the lady who is always found calmly seated in the best place, however great the crush is' (*90*).

89

PITTITES AT THE PLAY—THE YOUNG PEOPLE WHO LIKE
THE DARK SCENES

PITTITES AT THE PLAY—THE OLD GENTLEMAN FROM THE COUNTRY

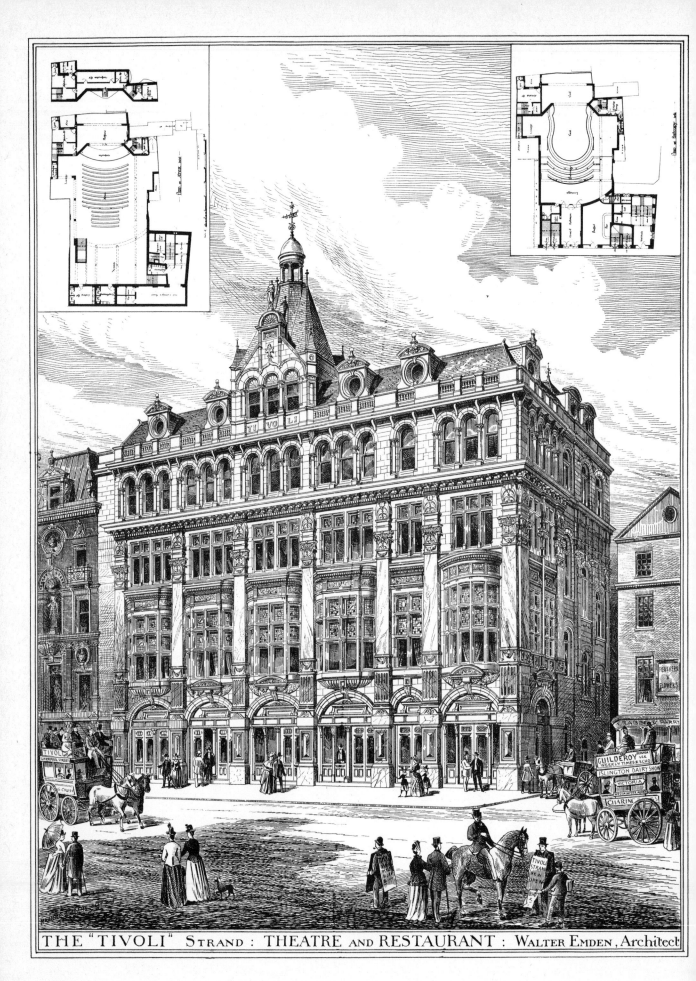

THE "TIVOLI" Strand : THEATRE and RESTAURANT : Walter Emden, Architect

Music hall grandeur: the Tivoli (1888–90)

During the 1880s the music hall became the
Theatre of Varieties, grander and more
respectable. The Alhambra became the Alhambra
Theatre of Varieties in 1884 and the Empire
followed suit in 1887. As they went over to music
hall, the houses were redecorated ever more
flamboyantly; the Tivoli (1888–90) was extremely
splendid. Emulating the Criterion in combining
theatre and restaurant, the building presented to the
Strand a gorgeous mixture: Plantagenet windows
were separated by a giant order of French Empire
pilasters, surmounted by an attic storey of
Romanesque arcading and topped by a Mansard
roof. Walter Emden, the architect, had in fact
conceived a similarly eclectic and extravagant
central feature for the roof (93), but unfortunately
this was omitted from the completed scheme as
seen here in 1890 (94).

Once again, the architect did not make provision
for advertising; as a result, the Neo-romanesque
style is somewhat obscured by the light-boxes
which spell out the name TIVOLI, while the clean
ground-floor lines are littered with prop-up
billboards.

The Strand elevation was in fact that of the
restaurant, while the theatre was behind (see plans,
93). The term 'variety' described not only the
kind of entertainment available but also the choice
of décor. The buffet, at street level, was in Indian
style. A staircase in François I style led to the Palm
Room (walls and ceiling decorated with palm
leaves) on the first floor and the Flemish Room
(oak carved in the Levant) on the second. Above
were suites of private dining-rooms, 'adorned in
styles which their names convey, namely – the
Louis XV Room, the Japanese, the Arabian and the
Pompeian Rooms; and in addition there is a
fair-sized Masonic Room'. The kitchens were
concealed behind the Romanesque arcading.

The Tivoli cost nearly £300,000, which was
expensive considering that the Palace, Cambridge
Circus, was done for £150,000 a little later. The
Tivoli Company went bankrupt within a year and
the building was sold for half its cost. Soon
afterwards a new Company was formed and the
theatre went on to become the most famous of
music halls.

94

Orientalizing

The Tivoli became so synonymous with variety that its style of decoration created a vogue which influenced music halls all over Britain. Tivolis were built across the Empire. The Alhambra, even when it was the Panopticon, had been Saracenic; when it was rebuilt in 1883, after the fire of the previous year, it was tempered with the Moorish of Spain. The Tivoli was Indian; gods and goddesses were carved in high relief, coloured and gilt, while the boxes were swagged with Baroque opulence (95) and elephants' heads topped the delicate iron columns supporting the ceiling. The elephant motif reappears in the Palace Music Hall, Glasgow (1907; 96, 97).

The Moorish-Indian style became very contagious. Frank Matcham redecorated the Tivoli slightly in 1891, just after this photograph was taken. The onion-shaped Moorish arches of the set, seen here, were a particular favourite of his; many of his Palaces of Variety sprouted onion domes in the 1890s (see Palace, Leeds, pp. 90, 91).

96

97

Early 1880s: increased capacities

During the late 1870s and 1880s the population grew rapidly and the proletariat became more prosperous. London stars on tour were increasingly highly paid and, if companies were not to stay too long in any one provincial city, theatre capacities had to be greater. The only way to do this without the better dress-circle seats being too far from the stage was to increase the depth of the pit and to deepen the balconies. Until the 1890s and the full development of the cantilever system, these balconies were supported on columns. Invariably,

each balcony was set back from the one below it (98), for otherwise the top of the proscenium arch would not be visible from the back seats. The worst seats, however, at the back of the immense galleries (always a feature of the British theatre) were a very long way from the stage (101); the Lyceum, Edinburgh, by Phipps (1883), demonstrates that although the entire proscenium opening could be seen the setting and actors looked microscopic (102, taken from same spot as previous shot). Even the beautiful ceiling was invisible (99).

99

100

101

102

103

104

Since its first opening, the Lyceum gallery has been reseated. Galleries at that time had simple steps, as in the Theatre Royal, York (*c.* 1882; *100*), or at best backed padded benches like the gallery in the Alhambra, Glasgow (1907; *103*). Each part of the house had its own entrance and separate staircase; customers dressed and smelled differently, and it was necessary to keep them apart. Galleryites had a long way to climb. (*104*) shows the long haul up to the gallery at York's Theatre Royal, which has been made more comfortable since these photographs were taken.

Audiences in the 1880s Theatre-going was jolly, festive and dressy, but not without its hazards, as these caricatures from *Ally Sloper's Half-Holiday* (105) indicate. Tootsie, the innocent to the left armed with fan and bouquet, noted in January 1888 that 'Papa [Ally Sloper] has taken a private box for the run of *Puss in Boots* [at Drury Lane], and some of the family are to be seen at the theatre every night. Papa says that he did it to do Gussie a good turn, but we don't believe it – he's always winking at some of the ladies of the ballet. One night he took Tottie, Lardi and Nellie, and it would have been a most successful evening had not Papa been hit in the eye with a turnip – accidentally, of course.' Apparently a telescope added to Ally's enjoyment of the aesthetic pleasures. Field-glasses were not without their uses, and the mirror in the stage box was convenient for last-minute repairs.

105

SLOPER AT DRURY LANE.

SLOPER AT SADLER'S WELLS.

106

Ally Sloper was constantly in trouble and Tootsie
(*106*, far right) was always at hand to describe his
misfortunes. 'Papa's at it again,' she reported the
following month. 'You'd hardly believe it, but he's
got a private box for the run of *Bluff King Hal* at
Sadler's Wells Theatre now, and members of the
Family are taken in turn to grace the performance
each evening. Mr George Roberts, the manager, is
awfully attentive to me, I know that. The other
night Bill Higgins upset Papa, and considerable
damage was done to the big drum, and also to
Uncle Boffin, who was mashing in the stalls.' Other
members of the Family were munching in the
stage box. A hip-flask came in handy, too;
Victorian propriety was not above enjoying
itself on a night out. By comparison, a modern
audience is far too docile.

The Garrick (1888–9)

In the late 1880s Phipps, with 40 theatres to his name, was rather in disgrace; his Theatre Royal, Exeter, had burnt down in 1887 with the loss of 140 lives and, though in mitigation the architect claimed that he had provided against fire, he admitted that he 'did not allow for smoke'. Younger architects rushed to take his place. His principal rival, Walter Emden, was appointed by W. S. Gilbert to design the Garrick; Phipps was still indispensable, however, and most of the execution was his. Later, he was denigrated by Sachs with the remark that 'he thought too little, designed and built too quickly', albeit his forte was 'clever planning under the most difficult circumstances'. The Garrick, completed in 1889, proved particularly troublesome. The site was awkward (107) and during construction an underground river, known to the Romans, started bubbling into the foundations. Nevertheless, the theatre opened on 24 April 1889 with Pinero's *The Profligate*, and it remains to this day virtually unchanged. The front elevation is rather deceptive. The auditorium runs parallel with Charing Cross Road and is partially masked by the lower well-articulated wall of rustication, pilasters and blind windows which connects the stage and the entrance colonnade. Internally, Phipps replaced his usual deep, narrow auditorium with a plain U-shape. The proscenium is created by the pilasters that frame the stage boxes (108 and colour plate III); this was a dramatic and simple change from the mock picture-frame of the Haymarket.

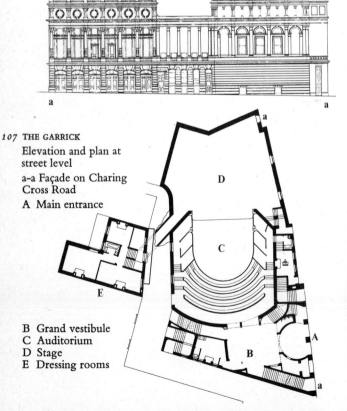

107 THE GARRICK
Elevation and plan at street level
a–a Façade on Charing Cross Road
A Main entrance
B Grand vestibule
C Auditorium
D Stage
E Dressing rooms

108

109

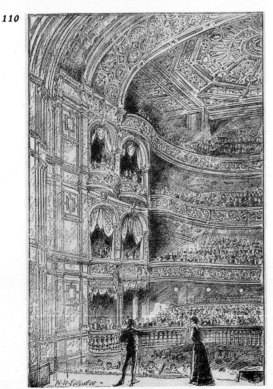

110

111

New technology: the Palace (1889–91)

D'Oyly Carte was a brave man. Besides coping with Gilbert and Sullivan, he eagerly embraced every new technical development and, not content with the success of the Savoy, started building his new Royal English Opera House in 1889. He worked with the master builder G. H. Holloway, and T. E. Collcutt, the Gothicist, was only summoned at a later stage to undertake the architectural elaboration. The new theatre opened on 31 January 1891 with Sullivan's *Ivanhoe*, to great acclaim. It was thought to be the best new theatre in Britain. Cantilevers, in modified form, were used in the Alhambra when it was rebuilt in 1883, but D'Oyly Carte's were 'unparalleled in any other theatre in Europe' (*110*). Far below the stage its own current was manufactured; 'with its 2,000-odd lights it has the largest theatrical installation in the world'. The 'electro-motors' also supplied the house with 'fresh air, passed over ice in summer and hot-water pipes in winter. Stale air was electrically extracted', a very early use of full air-conditioning.

Collcutt had clothed the building in an intricate fenestrated screen of brick and terracotta tiles, 'the climax of the Reign of Terracotta', as Sir Albert Richardson called it (*109*). Their ornament is Plateresque, the style of the early Spanish Renaissance (*111*).

But D'Oyly Carte's dream was short-lived. By December 1892, the Opera House had been sold to Augustus Harris and it reopened as the Palace Theatre of Varieties (*112*).

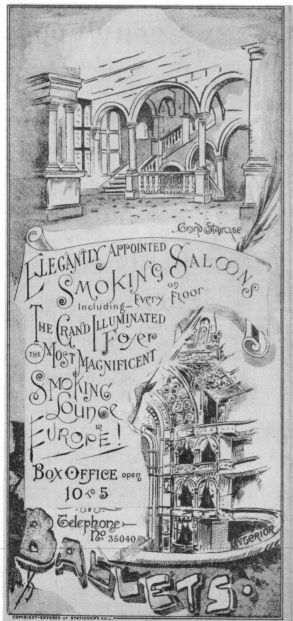

The Empire Music Hall, Newcastle upon Tyne (1891)

To illustrate and describe only the seminal, new and expensive theatres of the period would be misleading. Hundreds of new theatres were built around the country in a traditional and well-loved manner, and the work of local architects such as Oliver and Leeson in Newcastle had a remarkable assurance and control. No cantilevers here, but the simplest rectangle containing two tiers supported by iron columns, one lyre-shaped, the other squared off parallel to the outside wall – a late but not unusual hangover from the concert hall period of music hall design. The applied decoration was rich and powerful: Flemish Renaissance strapwork at the proscenium, adjacent to walls covered in Lincrusta paper, the whole made cosy and homely by gilt-framed mirrors and neatly-placed pictures (*113*).

113

115

116

'114

The exterior of the Empire was in the style of the early Flemish Renaissance (*114*); a façade that was preserved by Matcham when he made over the auditorium in 1901. The rich and comfortable cosiness extended to all parts of the house and even the corridors had a plush domestic quality. (*118*) shows the entrance to the balcony slips; fortunately there was never a panic here, for the table (right foreground) would have presented a splendid hazard. Note too the jute runner covering the carpet in the corridor and the first-class bar (*115*); the management was house-proud.

Music hall bars were exceptionally profitable, a fact which was openly recognized by their owners, and as a result better accommodation was provided than at many West End theatres. (*116*) shows the first-class bar parlour, which has a Spanish flavour with its richly-tooled imitation leather dado and its riotously patterned carpet, ceiling and wall panels *à la* William Morris. The naked incandescent light-bulbs must have been glaring, though the first-class bar has gas jets as well.

The *pièce de résistance* of the auditorium was its superb ceiling (*117*). A central saucer dome of Flemish strapwork is surrounded by a lattice-work border, touched with gilt. Five electroliers enliven the whole. The Empire was unusual in having no gallery; it had instead private boxes at the upper balcony level, probably indicating that the audience was of one social class, divided only by slight financial distinctions. The most expensive seats were the padded stalls, followed by the boxes with loose chairs, the less padded dress circle, finally the undivided pit benches and, in the Empire, the balcony slips and upper slips.

117, 118

THE Building has been erected on the latest and most up-to-date lines, from the designs and under the immediate supervision of that Eminent Theatrical Architect, Mr. FRANK MATCHAM, of London. The whole Building is Luxuriously Furnished and Upholstered, the Seating comfortable and so arranged that everyone obtains a clear and uninterrupted view of the Stage, the whole being carried out in perfect taste and harmony. The FINE ENTRANCES from Briggate, containing lofty Vestibules with Walls, Columns, and Staircases of Italian Marble, Balconies, and enriched Dome Ceilings, give some idea of the magnificence beyond. Lounges, Foyers, Saloons, and Smoking Rooms are provided with Retiring Rooms, and every accommodation for the comfort of the Audience has been studied.

High Class Music and Varieties

INTERIOR

119

The Empire Palace Music Hall, Leeds (c. 1897)

One of H. E. (later Sir Edward) Moss's famous Empire Palaces. The original Empire Palace opened in Edinburgh in 1892 with fantastic success, largely due to its architect Frank Matcham. His technical virtuosity in providing just what was required led

to the chain of music halls in provincial cities which
were incorporated in 1899 as Moss' Empires
Limited. It is interesting to note that this programme
of 1903 still extols the theatre, and its architect, as
one of its main attractions (*119*).

"THE FLYING SCUD" AT THE THEATRE ROYAL.

120

121

122

Imperial copies

Theatres of one sort or another were common in the British Colonies from the early days of the Empire. On occasion, intrepid English actors had voyaged forth; it took Gustavus Vaughan Brooke eighty-five days to reach Melbourne in 1855, performing in Cape Town on the way. By the 1890s colonial globe-trotting was usual, and stars of the West End made the lucrative passage to a chain of theatres of varying standards which flourished across the Empire. Invariably, theatres were influenced by and in some cases were copies of those at 'home'. Transatlantic ties were even closer, but from the end of the eighteenth century American theatre architecture had branched off from the British in its own direction and, by the 1850s, theatres there were as different from those in Britain as from theatres in Italy or Germany.

Cape Town had seen a dozen little makeshift theatres by the time the Theatre Royal was built in 1875. It burned down in 1883, but was rebuilt in 1884 (120, 121) before it burned down again in 1888. The post-gold-rush Opera House (1893; 122) was far more sumptuous. Italianate in a rather endearing late-nineteenth-century English Colonial manner, it was distinguished by sensible cast-iron verandas, typical of South African urban building at this time.

124

(123) The Theatre at Maritzburg, c. 1895

125

Adjustment to climatic conditions was not much in evidence in the other Imperial examples illustrated here: the Theatre Royal, Melbourne (1872; 124), the Princess Theatre, Melbourne (1886), by William Pitt (125) and the Gaiety, Bombay (126). The Theatre Royal, built after the Gold Rush and on occasion seating about 3,500, was internally very much in the style of the current Drury Lane and externally would be at home in any English street scene of the 1870s. The Princess, on the other hand has intimations of that breadth of vision which culminated in the fantasy and extravagance of the Sydney Opera House.

126

Private theatres in the 1890s

Britain does not share the Continental tradition of private theatres attached to the great stately homes; the Margravine of Anspach's little theatre at Brandenburg House (1792) and Wyatville's ballroom-theatre at Chatsworth (c. 1820s) are among the few. Private theatricals, however, were very popular, but for these the custom was to erect a temporary curtained stage at one end of the largest room in the house.

For thirty years, during the Queen's mourning, no theatrical performances took place at Windsor, but in 1891 the Waterloo Chamber was fitted up and the Savoy production of *The Gondoliers* was performed (*127*). The lush vegetation must have impaired the Royal party's view somewhat, and in subsequent years they were mounted up on a railed dais; (*128*) shows the command performance of *La Navarraise* by the Royal Opera Company in 1894.

Adelina Patti was more ambitious. After buying Craig-y-Nos Castle, near Swansea, she and her husband, the tenor Nicolini, installed electricity (said to have been the first in a private house) and in 1891 built their own little theatre attached to the castle (*129*). It was essentially a ballroom with a permanent stage and an orchestra pit seating twenty at one end; the wooden floor was so constructed that it could be tilted up to improve the sightlines. Patti entertained her guests with highlights from her career. The little theatre still exists (*130, 131*), along with its original scenery, including an act drop painted by Hawes Craven of Semiramide in a Roman chariot, with the face of La Diva herself (see colour plate IV).

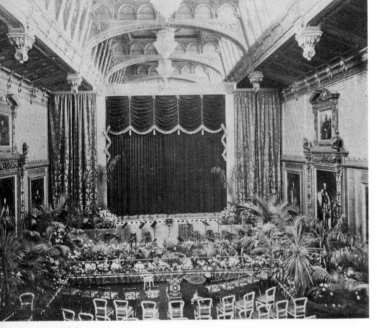

127

128

THE THEATRE.

A VIEW IN THE GARDEN.

INAUGURATION OF THE PATTI THEATRE AT CRAIG-Y-NOS.

THE EXTERIOR OF THE PATTI THEATRE.

SIGNOR NICOLINI.

MADAME ADELINA PATTI NICOLINI.

129

130

131

132

INTERIOR OF PAVILION GRAND PIER.

WESTON
SUPER MARE

THE PAVILION & BAND-STAND, GRAND PIER.

133

Piers, pavilions, Kursaals, etc.

The 'show at the end of the pier' was an essential
part of Victorian theatrical life (*132*), giving many
people their first experience of the theatre, and
actors, particularly music hall artists, their first jobs.
At first the piers were purely functional: the
beautiful Brighton Chain Pier (1823) was originally
built to accommodate the ever-increasing passenger
traffic between England and France. With the
growing popularity of seaside holidays, the piers
became the landlubber's opportunity of going to
sea, without the nausea. Pavilions, containing
all-purpose concert hall theatres, restaurants and all
the fun of the fair, soon followed. Hundreds of
these very British follies of nautical engineering
were erected around the coast.

The Britannia Pier, Great Yarmouth (1858; *134*),
is typical of the short pier, with a structure at the
tip highly reminiscent of the Music Hall in the
Surrey Zoological Gardens (see p. 47). Internally,
the arrangement of the theatres was also in the
manner of the early music halls – a flat floor with a
stage at one end and a single balcony round the
other three sides of the room – such as that of the
pier theatre at Weston-super-Mare (*133*) and the
Pavilion at Kingstown, now Dun Laoghaire (*136,
137*). Often the multi-purpose hall had a stage on
the long wall, as in the Palace Ballroom, Douglas,
Isle of Man (*138*).

In the more prosperous resorts, these
entertainment centres were conceived in the most
sumptuous style. The ballroom of Blackpool's
famous Tower Pavilion uses the Baroque opulence
of 'nineties theatre architecture with astonishing
flamboyance (*139*). In the same building the
permanent circus displayed equal vigour, but in the
Alhambresque style.

Kursaals, as their name implies, were of
Continental origin. Few of the British specimens
were quite as splendid as the casino/entertainment
centre/spa palaces to be found at the elegant
watering-places across the Channel. Harrogate,
however, as one of the most fashionable of English
spas, was well equipped with a Kursaal of suitable
extravagance (*140, 141*).

134

Britannia Pier, Gt. Yarmouth.

135

SOUTHSEA. THE PIER

136

The Pavilion, Kingstown. Co. Dublin.

137

138

Palace Ballroom, Douglas, I.O.M.

139

140

HARROGATE.

INTERIOR OF KURSAAL
HARROGATE

141

The 'nineties were a busy time for theatre architects. Shaftesbury Avenue, completed in 1886, was acquiring its complement of theatres. This 1897 view (*142*) shows the London Pavilion, which opened in 1885 (right), followed by the Trocadero (1882); on the north-west side is Phipps's Lyric of 1888, while further up (not seen here) were the Palace (1891) and the Shaftesbury (1888), which was bombed in the war. Still to be built were the Apollo (1901), the Globe (1906), the Queen's (1907) and the Prince's (1911), now the Shaftesbury.

Round the corner in Cranbourn Street was Daly's (1891–3). Built by George Edwardes of the Gaiety for the American impresario Augustin Daly, it housed the most famous musicals of the day. The French Renaissance front of lush yellow stone (*143*), designed by Spencer Chadwick with Phipps's assistance, set a new standard of opulence for the West End. The interior, instead of the usual pale delicate colouring, was a riot of 'ruby, Venetian red, dull silver and burnished gold', a herald of the plush and gold of the next two decades.

The Hippodrome (1899–1900; *144–6*), next to Daly's (extreme left on (*146*), a 1902 photograph), was erected by Moss (of the Empires). By this time his architect, Frank Matcham, had built him umpteen music halls up and down the country; here the commission was for a circus/water-spectacle/music hall. Circus-theatres and hippodromes had been very popular throughout the nineteenth century, both in Britain and on the Continent. In London, Matcham combined his typical rectangular plan, with its ornamental niches and straight-sided balconies, with a central circus arena poised on hydraulic rams. For *naumachiae* (water-spectacles) the lowest level of the arena could be flooded with 100,000 gallons of water from the Cran Bourne which conveniently flows under the stage (*145*). High-divers could plunge from the balustraded central dome, which opened to reveal the starry night, and twenty elephants could slide down a chute into the water. When animals were used, the arena was enclosed with steel railings 12 feet high. Just before the Hippodrome was changed into a straightforward Palace of Varieties in 1909, by bringing the proscenium forward and filling in the arena with removable seats, a show called *The Arctic* featured 70 polar bears.

For a theatre supposed to accommodate 3,000, the front-of-house facilities were minimal. An entrance vestibule led into an oval foyer (*144*), connected to the Cabin, a bar designed to resemble an ocean liner.

The Hippodrome was revamped as the Talk of the Town in 1958.

142

London.
Daly's Theatre,
Leicester Square.

143

144

145

146

1890s: suburban pretension

Theatre life in London was not all West End. Every borough, every High Street had by this time one, two or more theatres and music halls. In her reference book *London Theatres and Music Halls 1850–1950*, Diana Howard lists 910 separate institutions, many of which saw countless alterations of name and fabric.

Frank Matcham's office spawned other theatre specialists. Two of them, Bertie Crewe and W. G. R. Sprague, designed the Metropole in Camberwell (1894) for J. B. Mulholland, an obsessive 'man of the theatre' who not only owned and managed his own house but directed and partly wrote his pantomimes; his portrait appeared on the programme for the fourth, *Little Red Riding Hood*, in 1897 (*147*). The vignettes of the theatre show the architects to be still much influenced by their elders. The auditorium, with its frilly proscenium and the frieze of Moorish round horseshoe multifoil arches, could be Matcham, while the exterior might be Phipps at his most prosaic.

Within a few years, however, Sprague had matured into the most interesting and versatile theatre architect of the period. The Balham Hippodrome (1899; *148*) had a superbly bombastic mannerist extravagance gloriously suited to its function: this building could only be a music hall. Perhaps Sprague paid for it himself; he was certainly the licensee, which at the time meant 'actual and responsible manager', in 1900 and again in 1904.

The architect as theatre-speculator was not an unusual phenomenon. Sachs maintains that 'with but a few exceptions . . . it is the architect who is the prime mover in the transaction', who acquired the land, made the plans and found the backers. Today, this would be highly unethical.

150

West End elegance: Her Majesty's (1896–7)

Beerbohm Tree's new Her Majesty's opened on 28 April 1897, a month before the death of Phipps, its architect; his grandest building was to be his monument. Sachs, in his *Modern Opera Houses and Theatres*, though caustic about Phipps's shortcomings, was also generous in his praise:

With his departure we have lost a man who had excelled in his speciality to an extent that can scarcely be understood by an outsider. He had been able to satisfy the requirements of the typical theatrical speculator, who primarily demands the greatest accommodation in a limited space at as low a cost as possible, and what is more, he enjoyed full confidence, since no one had cause to fear any inclination on his part to incur expenditure merely in the interests of art. . . . Her Majesty's Theatre is the outcome of the practical financial ability of the late C. J. Phipps; for the development of the large site, on which the theatre only occupies a section, is practically due to his management.

Two-thirds of the site previously completely occupied by the Novosielski Nash/Repton Opera House (see pp. 26, 27) was allotted to the Carlton Hotel (seen on the right, at the far end of the Haymarket, *150*). The sensible combination of theatre and hotel dates back in Britain to Foulston's Theatre Royal and Royal Hotel in Plymouth (1811–13). Phipps gave good value for money; Her Majesty's cost a mere £60,000, as against the £150,000 of the Palace and nearly £300,000 of the Tivoli earlier in the decade. The massive pile of Portland stone oozes wealth and prosperity. Its French Renaissance style is that of the Second Empire: a compendium of architectural gems from the Louvre. Tree claimed that the auditorium – in which he had quite some say – was Louis XIV (*149, 151*), but in fact it was Louis XV. Its stylish gilt and marbled-plaster recalls, in diluted form, Gabriel's Opéra Royal de Versailles, completed in 1770, while the giant order framing the royal box is an exact copy of that in Gabriel's masterpiece. It was a fit setting for Edward VII and Queen Alexandra, seen here at the first night of *Herod* in 1902 (*152*).

151

152

153

154

West End elegance: Wyndham's (1899)

When W. G. R. Sprague built the grandiose Balham Hippodrome (*148*) in 1899, he was also working on Wyndham's, the first of his many small and elegant West End theatres which, happily, still survive. It is perhaps not generally realized that almost all of London's superbly intimate turn-of-the-century playhouses were designed by one man; Sprague was the architect of Wyndham's (1899), the Albery (1903; see colour plate VI), the Strand (1905), the Aldwych (1905), the Globe (1906), the Queen's (1907), the Ambassadors (1913) and the St Martin's (1916). He also designed several other theatres in the London area, most of which have been destroyed. The Coronet (1898), now the Gaumont Cinema in Notting Hill Gate, and the Camden (1901) in Camden Town still survive, though under threat of demolition. The Edward VII in Paris, though apparently extremely French, was also designed by Sprague.

As a comparative analysis of what a really competent architect can achieve when working within an accepted tradition, I have grouped together four of Sprague's theatres (pp. 104–11) regardless of their chronology. It must be stressed here that production style, audience expectations, kind of audience and social milieu were all totally predictable.

Smart London at the time, Sprague included, was intensely Francophile; yet though Sprague's architecture was eclectic it blended various styles with masterful assurance into a very personal and well-balanced whole. No matter what the derivation of his West End theatres, they are supreme examples of late Edwardian–Victorian London. Wyndham's is the smallest of those illustrated here; it now seats 769, but when it opened it accommodated about 1,200 people: 540 on satin-upholstered tip-up chairs, the rest on undivided pit and gallery benches (*155*). To accentuate the intimacy, a boudoir version of Louis XVI was chosen. The ceiling paintings were a *fin de siècle* rendering of Boucher.

The picture-frame proscenium, one of the last of its kind remaining in London, is surmounted by a bust which is reputedly of Mary Moore, Charles Wyndham's leading lady and later his wife. She is flanked by various admirers: Sheridan, Goldsmith and two winged adolescents (*153*). The plaster palm fronds were apparently insufficient for the Wyndham family, who suburbanized Sprague's meticulous finish with a few potted specimens, both in the auditorium and in the saloon (*154*). The photographs were taken by Bedford Lemière soon after the opening of the theatre.

West End elegance: the Aldwych (1905)

Though the decoration of the Aldwych was described in contemporary press releases as Georgian, it is in fact a mixture of Georgian and French Baroque-classicism (*156*). None of the Sprague theatres illustrated here had Daly's red and plush intensity which is now considered synonymous with the period. Wyndham's was turquoise-blue, cream, gilt and *vieux rose*; the Aldwych crimson, cream and gold, with rose du Barry upholstery and draperies; the Globe rose du Barry, ivory and gold; and the Queen's white and gold with green carpets, hangings and upholstery.

The Aldwych is a twin of the Strand Theatre, which was originally called the Waldorf; their identical façades, beautifully adapted to their corner sites, are separated by the Waldorf Hotel. The entire block forms an impressive and unified whole, something typical of the Aldwych–Kingsway scheme, which was one of the projects that in the early years of the twentieth century transformed Georgian and mid-Victorian London into an Imperial capital.

Electric candles with silk shades were already fashionable for wall sconces. The naked bulbs of the 'nineties which gave a harsh and unflattering light were soon shaded to make the light more soothing, though the central chandeliers that tended to give a flat dead light to the auditorium were still used (*161*).

By 1905, stage lighting was entirely electrical. As the action took place *within* the proscenium frame, lighting equipment was confined to battens in the flies, in the footlights and in the wings. With the invention of projector lamps in 1914, the earlier hand-controlled arc spotlights could be superseded by 'remote-control' spots. After about 1922 this system was much improved and spotlights were gradually moved out into the auditorium. Older theatres had of course no special provision for these spotlights, which had to be tacked on to balcony fronts and around the side boxes, spoiling the exquisite architectural completeness illustrated in these early photographs. At Covent Garden, the beauty of the theatre is respected and the spots are kept backstage and behind sliding panels in the ceiling. Sprague's work at the Aldwych, moreover, has been blurred further since the Royal Shakespeare Company took over the theatre in 1960 and brought a forestage forward to the line of the stage boxes, with an electric batten and a curtain border above, thus upsetting the sightlines from many seats. Painting the entire theatre dark olive, however, but leaving the gilt ornament intact, has created an atmosphere more suitable to production styles of today, certainly not to the theatre's detriment.

◁ *156*

West End elegance: the Globe (1906)

The Globe is separated from its twin, the Queen's, by a commercial block with shops. Although the two theatres were externally identical, inside Sprague manifested his virtuosity (*157*, *158*, *160*, *161*).

The Globe's predominant Baroque-classicism is again married to Georgian. The stage boxes were unfortunately reshaped in 1930, when 'modernistic' light-fittings (seen in these photographs of 1943) were installed; however, the damage was slight. The sense of enveloping decoration is still dynamic. By enriching the wall surfaces behind the spectators, the architect avoids the great areas of bleakness so disturbing in most post-war theatres. Knowing what to do with a wall is the essence of the traditional theatre; the audience, when surrounded by itself and by decoration, seems to focus its attention on the stage. This apparent paradox, which has nevertheless been demonstrated time and time again, creates the 'theatrical atmosphere' which exists in these brilliantly vivacious auditoria.

Apart from the incongruous light-fittings, the foyer (*158*) is a worthy entrance to the theatre: a beautiful example of an architect supremely confident in his handling of space and decoration. By opening up the ground-floor ceiling into the first-floor saloon, a sense of great spaciousness has been created in what is in fact a very small area.

158

The new elegance of the West End theatre was very much part of the social scene. Theatre-going preceded the great private soirées or 'dining in style' at one of the grand hotels or restaurants. The caption to this drawing (*159*) from *The Sphere* (20 August 1904) reads: '... The reconstructions at the Savoy Hotel make it one of the finest buildings in London, while the enlarged space given to the restaurant is greatly in favour of the guests.'

AFTER THE THEATRE
The Entrance to the Foyer of the Savoy Restaurant.

159

West End elegance: the Queen's (1907)

The Queen's provides an extraordinary conglomeration of styles and elements: Italian Cinquecento (the order, pilasters and arches over the stage boxes and the frieze over the proscenium), Robert Adam (the balcony fronts), early Georgian (the acoustic cove above the proscenium; *160*), and Edwardian Baroque (the luscious ceiling; *161*). The plaster figure-work complicates the amalgam even further: the putti on the balcony fronts resemble Donatello's, while the abandoned Bacchantes on the abutments above the pilasters are Art Nouveau and the muscular creatures on the ceiling are as androgynous as the favourites of Michelangelo. Yet the entire composition works superbly. Particularly clever are the boxes set into the wall above the dress circle, filling the space which has resulted from good sectional planning; when this balcony is sufficiently raked to provide good sightlines, its back row would have its view cut if the second

balcony were brought too low. In the Globe the side wall, often too dominant, is articulated with coupled columns interspersed with niches, doors, swags and cartouches.

The Shaftesbury Avenue front of the Queen's was badly damaged during the war. In 1958 a new elevation and new front-of-house accommodation of quite painful banality were erected by Messrs Westwood, Sons and Partner, assisted by Sir Hugh Casson. Fortunately the auditorium remained more or less unscathed and was restored in red, gold and white.

When the Queen's opened in 1907, J. E. Vedrenne, the licensee, made a prophetic decision: seven shillings and sixpence were to be charged for the first three rows of the dress circle and five shillings for the next eight rows, 'in which evening dress will be optional'. It was a sign of the ending of an era.

West End elegance: the Imperial (1901)

Frank T. Verity was even more more Francophile
than Sprague. When he took over his father's
architectural practice (see pp. 66–9), he contributed
to the firm of Thomas Verity & Son his own
Beaux-Arts training and solemn admiration of
Garnier's Paris Opéra.

In 1900 Lily Langtry bought the lease of the
Imperial, which had opened in 1876 as the Royal
Aquarium Theatre, a part of the immense Royal
Aquarium Summer and Winter Garden, opposite
Westminster Abbey. Financed by her current
paramour, Edgar Cohen, she had Verity completely
reconstruct the interior (162, 163). The result was a
somewhat chilly and almost over-pure Empire
style, contrasting strongly with Sprague's intense,
all-enveloping theatricality and professionalism.
Two steep balconies face a Greek temple, while on
either side marble walls are dominated by a pair
of superbly detailed royal boxes. Mrs Langtry was
not, after all, suffering from *folie de grandeur*; her
association with the King was well-known. For a
command performance in 1902, the year after the
theatre opened, both he and Queen Alexandra
(164), along with the Prince and Princess of Wales,
occupied these royal boxes.

In theatre-architectural terms, however, the
fashion for detached boxes set by the Imperial was
not a happy one. The former relationship between
audience and actor was visually interrupted; it was
the beginning of the problem of dissociation which
became most acute in the cinema era.

Despite her grand connections, Mrs Langtry had
no luck with the Imperial, and the command
performance was her last there. New horizons were
in view, however; the era of the director who
brought fresh conceptions to the theatre was
beginning. In 1903 William Poel and his
Elizabethan Stage Society performed *Everyman* at
the Imperial, and Ellen Terry presented her son
Gordon Craig's revolutionary productions of *The
Vikings* and *Much Ado About Nothing*.

The Imperial was dismantled in 1906, and its
interior was taken off to Canning Town to
refurbish the old Royal Albert Music Hall, which
opened as the Imperial Palace and was destroyed by
fire in 1931.

The enormous Central Hall, which opened in
1912, now stands on the site of the Royal Aquarium
and Imperial Theatre.

162

163

164

West End elegance: the Playhouse (1905–6)

The strong contrast in the Playhouse between the neat, well-mannered exterior and the demented vulgarity of the interior – the marvellous *brio* of the music hall sweeping into the straight theatre – arises from its curious and dramatic history. This is the building, mentioned on p. 39, which was originally erected in 1881–2 by Sefton Parry in the hope that the South-Eastern Railway would have to buy him out. They did not; in 1905, however, the original architect F. H. Fowler rebuilt the theatre and part of Charing Cross Station promptly fell upon it even before the first night! One of Parry's successors, Cyril Maude, got the compensation. Most of Fowler's façade remained undamaged (*165*, right), but new architects, Detmar Blow and Fernand Billerey, reconstructed the interior in 1906 (*166*, *167*). Here we have another example of the stage box, this time *demi-mondaine* rather than royal, barely attached to the balconies. Intrusive walls are starting to appear, masked with illogical but highly amusing decoration. None of Sprague's suave control here; note, for instance, how the second balcony pierces the pansified picture on the wall!

165

166

167

The apotheosis of the music hall:
the London Coliseum (1904)

Music hall, as the very essence of show-biz, bred personalities larger than life, brash entrepreneurs with the splendid courage of the property speculators of our time; the former, however, were served by better architects who were working in an age when, no matter what the pretension or the pomposity, there was always room for fantasy and a human scale.

In 1902, when he decided to build a theatre bigger and better than London's largest, Drury Lane, Oswald Stoll at 35 was already, like his partners and rivals Moss, Thornton and Butt, the controller of a chain of music halls around the provinces. Frank Matcham, invariably their architect, designed the Coliseum, which opened on 24 December 1904 (*171*). It combined, as the programme trumpeted, 'the social advantages of the refined and elegant surroundings of a Club; the comfort and attractiveness of a Cafe, besides being the THEATRE DE LUXE OF LONDON and the pleasantest family resort imaginable'. Its seating capacity depended on where it was advertised, ranging between the 4,000 mentioned in the caption to this drawing from the *Sphere* and the 3,389 given out for licensing purposes. It now seats 2,354, plus 40 standing, and the audience can hear and see perfectly from the worst seats in the house.

When the Coliseum opened, four performances daily were planned, at 12 noon, 3 p.m., 6 p.m. and 9 p.m. Even the cheapest seats, costing sixpence in the balcony (never called the gallery), were bookable. Telegrams could be despatched, stamps sold, messages taken and sent. The royal box (*168*) was connected to the royal entrance by a carriage gliding smoothly on rails; it never worked! Nor for that matter did the four daily performances, which were soon cut down to two. A booking charge of sixpence was levied, and it was no longer possible to book balcony seats. Nonetheless, the best performers were persuaded to appear in variety: Ellen Terry, the Vanbrugh sisters, contingents from the Russian ballet and many others. Fantastic spectacles were presented on the immense revolving stage, 75 feet in diameter, containing three turntables which revolved independently. Horses raced round against them, and at one point a jockey was actually killed. Sarah Bernhardt appeared in Racine's *Phèdre* in 1913, a performance attended by King George and his family who sat in the stage box (*170*); presumably the royal box at the back of the stalls (*169*) was too far from the stage and less visible to the audience. The theatre has regained its magnificent viability today as the home of the English National Opera (*172–4*).

168, 169

170

△ 172, 173, 174

Touring houses: the King's, Glasgow (1904)

Matcham was not only a designer of music halls. By the turn of the century he had built scores of theatres of every type and size, and had remodelled and modernized dozens of others. He was able to offer a speedy and inexpensive solution to any commission because he had patented his own system of curvilinear cantilevers for balconies, slung between parallel walls, and his own concoctions of fibrous plaster.

His professionalism was well tailored to the needs of a booming and well-organized theatre industry. Pre-London tours of potentially profitable shows and post-London tours of acknowledged successes went out to chains of theatres across the country. The system of carefully

grouping the touring houses into three categories has continued into the television era, although it is now in decline. 'Try-outs', if they happen at all, are today extremely limited, while post-London touring is only sporadic.

The King's, being a Number 1 Touring, shows Matcham in a somewhat subdued and dignified vein. Broken pediments had become his trademark; a Matcham theatre invariably has them above the boxes and here one surmounts the proscenium too (176). The conches, used in the Coliseum above the stage boxes (170), become in the King's the main feature of the side walls at gallery level (175).

179

177

178

Touring houses: the King's, Edinburgh (1906)

The art of not disclosing too much too soon was well understood by Edwardian theatre architects. Messrs James Davidson of Coatbridge and J. D. Swanson of Kirkcaldy were canny Scots who tantalized their audience with dexterity. From outside, the King's in Edinburgh could be any sort of commercial building, an insurance company, for instance, but hardly a theatre (*179*). It is dour and solid, though prosperous, and is more suited to Glasgow's canyons of Victorian commercial acumen than Edinburgh's graceful propriety. Inside the main entrance, foyers and staircases mellow slightly into the good taste of a gentlemen's club (*177*). But once inside the auditorium! An Aladdin's cave of Viennese Baroque, swathed in all the plush and gilt of *la belle époque* at its fruitiest. Delightful! (*180* and colour plate VII.)

Certainly, these teasers from Coatbridge and Kirkcaldy have not measured up to the professionalism of the old hands like Sprague and Matcham. The towering range of boxes does not really marry with the balconies; the outermost mask-holding term is buffeted on the hip by the dress circle, and the gallery cuts into the ornament on a pilaster quite arbitrarily (*178*). The sightlines from the boxes, particularly the uppermost, are poor. But what is lacking in expertise is made up in exuberance. This was the 'illiterate Baroque' against which purists in the next decade were to rebel and by their pedantry emasculate a wonderful world of fantasy.

181

Contemporary viability

Although I have tried to point to the general new developments and changes which took place decade by decade during the Victorian and Edwardian period, it must be remembered that these changes were taking place in the more important theatres of the larger cities. In smaller towns, little theatres were being built which were almost dateless. The house illustrated here (*181–6*) could have been erected in Britain at any time after the 1850s, and on the Continent at any point during a period of 250 years; it was in fact built in Dublin in 1909. The photographs, taken in 1964 when the Abbey Theatre was being rebuilt and the Company was playing at the Queen's (*181*), attempt to demonstrate the complete viability for contemporary usage of these dynamically intimate playhouses. Few modern theatres can match the sense of excitement, the feeling for occasion and the total involvement between actor (*182*) and audience which are so pronounced in this little auditorium. In practical terms, more people are packed in closer to the actor than they could ever be in a post-war open-stage theatre – and they see and hear much better. The Queen's was demolished in 1968 to make way for an office block.

184

182

185

187

188

189

The beginning of the end

Theatre architecture achieved a magnificent flowering during the reigns of Victoria and Edward VII. It died with the growth of the cinema and the rise of the theatre director bringing new ideas about staging and theatrical forms. Previously, those working in the theatre had been perfectly content with the traditional buildings that they knew and loved; professional theatre architects provided just what was wanted. But the revolutionaries were bored with conventional theatre, and the gilt, plush and cherubs gave them claustrophobia. The conception of theatre as a social event, of audiences enjoying themselves in a world of fantasy, irritated and disturbed them. The 'message' of their plays was being swamped by what they considered to be giddy artificiality.

Wagner heralded the new trend. The audience at the Bayreuth Festspielhaus (1876) was forced to look directly at his closely integrated music-dramas and to ignore itself. But the sightlines from the sides of his wide fan-shaped auditorium were bad, and the next step was to chop off the sides, as in the Künstlertheater in Munich (1908). The first example of this style of auditorium in England was in the Little Theatre, John Adam Street (*187*), in 1910. There are no frills here – the play's the thing! It seems somehow fitting that this doctrinaire approach should, in London, have been interwoven with Suffragettism. Miss Gertrude Kingston, the 'onlie begetter' of the Little, was an ardent feminist and an equally ardent admirer of Max Reinhardt and all things German. In the form and spirit of the theatre, she acknowledged her debt to the great innovator with a stage cyclorama and its *Horizont* lighting. 'Delightful specimens of German art' decorated the walls of the foyer.

The directional theatre, with no side boxes or balconies, was of course eminently suited to the cinema. The earliest buildings erected specifically as cinemas naturally took this form; the Majestic Picturedrome, Tottenham Court Road (1910; *188, 189*), which remains intact as the Continentale,

could almost be the Little Theatre or, for that matter, any assembly hall anywhere. The Palace Cinema, Kentish Town (1913; *191*), is still related to the hall, yet with its proscenium arch and charmingly otiose caryatids smacks of a ballroom theatre like Adelina Patti's at Craig-y-nos (see p. 95). The Cinematograph Theatre, Finsbury Park (1915; *190*), albeit festooned with cherubs, gives intimation of a new fantasy; while harking back to the nineteenth century, this essentially cinematic dream culminated in the 'atmospheric' cinemas of the late 'twenties and early 'thirties, though this transatlantic innovation was experienced in Britain only in somewhat diluted guise. Instead, the great balloon-like structure, all balcony and wall, convex stalls and aridity became the rule as the cinema form. This in turn influenced theatre design, with disastrous effect, resulting in such horrors as the Cambridge, London (1930), and the new Shakespeare Memorial, Stratford-upon-Avon (1929–32).

Gargantuanism; the voluptuous turning hard: The Stoll (1910–11)

192

193

The immense wealth of Edwardian Britain, which architecturally speaking predates Edward VII's reign and continues for just over a decade after his death, gave rise to yet another phenomenon in theatre architecture: the building of ever larger theatres, inhuman and 'American' in scale.

Oscar Hammerstein I had conquered New York with a series of mammoth enterprises and so had decided to try his hand in London. By this he was, he asserted, 'paying the highest possible tribute to musical London, if not to England. My confidence in its musical taste and culture is unbounded.' Such high-flown enthusiasm characterized the booklet which contains Bertie Crewe's design (*192*) and which solicits custom for Hammerstein's London Opera House: 'Grand Opera can succeed only when it is presented "grand" in every detail; it must be "grand" in auditorium and on the stage; "grand" in singers, musicians, scenery and costumes; its Director and his staff must be imbued with the loftiest of purposes.' Within thirteen months, on 13 November 1911, Hammerstein's grand opera in Kingsway opened to the public with Nouguès and Cain's *Quo Vadis*, and by 13 July 1912, despite its projected repertoire of thirty-two operas, it had flopped. Competition from Covent Garden was too great; they had the most popular operas and the greatest singers under contract.

Bertie Crewe, another architect from Matcham's stable, had certainly echoed Hammerstein's ballyhoo. The elevation to Kingsway (*193*) was modelled on Perrault's great façade to the Louvre. Despite its claims to French Renaissance, however, the auditorium, which seated 2,420, shows other influences (*192*, *194*); the tier of boxes beneath the Grand Circle, a device new to England, was taken from the work of the great Viennese firm of theatre architects, Fellner and Helmer. Hammerstein had used this idea, combining it with the side walls of boxes surmounted by a great sounding-board, in one of the theatres in his Olympia (1895), on Broadway. In fact, the feel of the London Opera House is Central European, but via the United States, where Continental features and detailing were coarsened and enlarged out of all recognition.

Hammerstein, poorer by £47,000 (the building itself had cost him over £200,000), returned to New York, and the Opera House went over to variety and revue. In 1916 Oswald Stoll gained control and the following year turned it into a cinema, the Stoll Picture Theatre. The stage was still used for variety and orchestral turns preceding the film; such mixed programmes were very popular in the States, and in Britain until the 1950s.

Gargantuanism: the Shaftesbury (1911) and Golders Green Hippodrome (1913)

Bertie Crewe was one of the last of the great architects to specialize in theatre design; in his work we see the fire growing cold, the spirit diminishing. The Bedford Lemière photographs reproduced on these two pages and taken in 1912 and 1914 show how rapidly the decline took place.

The Shaftesbury, formerly the Prince's, opened as a blood-and-thunder house on 26 December 1911. The dynamic is still fiery and consistent. The side boxes, within their French Renaissance frontispiece, tie up beautifully with the two balconies; the plasterwork, although cheaply constructed, is deeper and richer than ever; the statuary is flamboyant and well-scaled (*195, 196*) – a suitable environment for the melodramas that were to fill the stage and thrill the popular audiences, who paid between sixpence and five shillings for the pleasure.

195

196

197

198

But in the Golders Green Hippodrome (1913; *197*),
which as a music hall should have been
equally vibrant, the temperature is lowered.
Certainly it is a larger house, seating 2,261 in 1969
as against the Shaftesbury's 1,500, but in 1911
Crewe had shown with the Stoll that he was
capable of handling a vast theatre. It was fashion,
not architectural ineptitude, which accounted for
the decline. The exterior of the theatre was dressed
up in the awkward and ham-fisted neo-Georgian
style which was then coming into vogue (*198*).
Inside, nothing convinces. The box facing towards
the audience is merely silly and had to be filled
with potted palms; the three-lioned chariot, above,
an almost identical copy of Matcham's at the
Coliseum, is far too small, and the sounding-board
above the proscenium is nude and overwhelming.
The overall decoration veers towards copybook
Roman, to the detriment of theatrical atmosphere.

Decline and fall

Perhaps it is right and proper that the decline of
Victorian and Edwardian theatre architecture, and
the pre-war society that it reflected, should have
been gowned in the trappings of ancient Rome and
Greece. It is no coincidence that there were so
many Royals, Palaces and Empires scattered about
Britain. The world that crashed in 1914–18 saw
itself very much in classical and imperial mould.

Definitely 1913 was Bertie Crewe's Roman
year. Besides building the tepid Golders Green
Hippodrome, he reconstructed the Palace,
Manchester (*199*, *201* and colour plate VIII), a
thriving music hall which first opened in 1891. It
is hardly credible that the same architect was
responsible for both theatres. Everything wrong
with the Golders Green is right with the Palace, yet
the effect is hard and cold and unsympathetic, the
Roman garb too accurate. The steeply-raked
balconies of padded chairs were eminently
comfortable, but from their front rows the vista is
stern and beneath them the sensation is oppressive.

202

Viewed under conditions like these, the poor little actor on stage is hardly credible to an audience crushed beneath the weight of the balcony (*201*), and after the invention of the cinema close-up the distant actor in the live theatre could no longer maintain his former attraction.

Even the sensitive Sprague was infected by the new fashion for a 'purer' Roman style. In his Penge Empire (*c.* 1914; the photograph (*200*) was taken in May 1915), one sees his touch freezing under the chill of this stern Classicism. Just as *real* flowers on stage are wrong and destroy illusion, so 'purity' in auditorium design becomes repellent, as it does in many modern theatres with their lavish and primly virginal use of natural materials such as plywood. Since the great tradition of illusion was swept away, many lessons have had to be learned all over again.

The final illustration shows a reconstruction by Wm and T. R. Milburn of the Empire, Cardiff, (1915–16; *202*), which seated 2,820 and had a great stalls audience on an almost flat floor, from which

there must have been an appalling view of the stage. This theatre, and others like it, close the Edwardian epoch and usher in the cinema age. Looking up at a cinema screen, the stalls would have been entertained; looking across between countless heads at a distant actor, they were frustrated. The decorative effect of the room has become so anaemic as to be almost invisible. The neo-Grecian features are so sparse as to be parsimonious; the boxes angled away from the stage are useless and irrelevant, no more than a mannerist remnant from a once vigorous tradition.

Fortunately for us, many superb theatre buildings from the Victorian and Edwardian era still survive. Though inevitably too many have gone, everything must be done to preserve those that remain. They have much to teach us; they continue to be eminently serviceable and practical; most important of all, their wonderful gaiety and vitality still remain to entrance us – and to gladden our hearts.

Further reading

This list is not intended as a full bibliography, but merely as an indication of a few books which cover certain aspects of the subject.

M. Baur-Heinhold, *Baroque Theatre*, London 1967.

R. J. Broadbent, *Annals of the Liverpool Stage*, Liverpool 1908.

F. Dangerfield (ed.), *The Playgoer*, vols. 1 and 2, London 1901–2.

D. Cheshire, *Music Hall*, Newton Abbot 1974.

R. Elkin, *The Old Concert Rooms of London*, London 1955.

J. Fleming, H. Honour, N. Pevsner, *The Penguin Dictionary of Architecture*, Harmondsworth 1972.

B. Gascoigne, *World Theatre*, London 1968.

P. Hartnoll (ed.), *The Oxford Companion to the Theatre*, third edition, London 1967.

H. R. Hitchcock, *Architecture: Nineteenth and Twentieth Centuries*, in the *Pelican History of Art* series, Harmondsworth 1958.

D. Howard, *London Theatres and Music Halls 1850–1950*, London 1970.

G. A. Jellicoe, *The Shakespeare Memorial Theatre*, London 1933.

R. Leacroft, *The Development of the English Playhouse*, London 1973.

R. Mander and J. Mitchenson, *The Lost Theatres of London*, London 1968.
—— *The Theatres of London*, London 1975.

B. McNamara, *The American Playhouse in the Eighteenth Century*, Cambridge, Mass. 1969.

D. C. Mullin, *The Development of the Playhouse*, Los Angeles 1970.

A. M. Nagler, *A Source Book in Theatrical History*, New York 1959.

D. Nalbach, *The King's Theatre 1704–1867*, London 1972.

N. Pevsner, *An Outline of European Architecture*, Harmondsworth 1963.

P. Roberts, *Theatre in Britain: A Playgoer's Guide*, London 1973.

E. Sachs, *Modern Opera Houses and Theatres*, in three vols., London 1896–8.

H. Scott, *The Early Doors*, London 1946.

F. H. W. Sheppard (ed.), *Survey of London*, particularly vol. XXXV, *The Theatre Royal, Drury Lane, and the Royal Opera House, Covent Garden*, and vols. XXXIII and XXXIV, *The Parish of St Anne, Soho*.

E. Sherson, *London's Lost Theatres of the XIX Century*, London 1925.

R. Southern, *The Georgian Playhouse*, London 1948.
—— *Changeable Scenery*, London 1952.

J. Summerson, *The Classical Language of Architecture*, London 1964.

Theatre Notebook: A Journal of the History and Technique of the British Theatre, London (began publication in 1945).

Theatre Survey: The American Journal of Theatre History, Pittsburgh (began publication in 1960).

R. Thorne, *Theatre Buildings in Australia to 1905*, in two vols., Sydney 1971.

S. Tidworth, *Theatres: An Illustrated History*, London 1973.

W. C. Young, *Documents in American Theater History*, in two vols., Chicago 1973.

Index

Numbers in *italic* refer to illustrations

Architects and designers

Architectural practices are listed as they appear in the text

Buildings

The term 'Royal' is omitted where it is a prefix (invariably meaningless) and is used only when it is the sole name of the theatre

Actors, Writers, Entrepreneurs, Directors, etc.